AFTERMATH

AFTERMATH
Surviving the Loss of God

John F. Crosby

Algora Publishing
New York

Library of Congress Cataloging-in-Publication Data —

Crosby, John F., 1955-
    Aftermath: surviving the loss of God / John F. Crosby.
        pages cm
    Includes bibliographical references and index.
        ISBN 978-0-87586-984-1 (pbk.: alk. paper) — ISBN 978-0-87586-985-8 (alk.
paper) — ISBN 978-0-87586-986-5 (ebook) 1. God. 2. Loss (Psychology)—
Religious aspects. 3. Religion—Controversial literature. I. Title.
    BL473.C76 2013
    211—dc23
                                    2013007689

Printed in the United States

For the brave and courageous who are breaking away.

Is he willing to prevent evil, but not able?
Then is he impotent.
Is he able, but not willing?
Then is he malevolent.
Is he both able and willing?
Whence then is evil? [1]

1 The question allegedly posed by Epicurus, 341–270 BCE, as formulated by David Hume in *Dialogues Concerning Natural Religion*, Part X. 1710. (New York: Barnes & Noble, 2006, p. 75.)

Table of Contents

Table of Contents

The purpose of this book is simple and straightforward. It is addressed to people like myself who can no longer embrace the idea of a god who is up there and out there looking after the welfare and well-being of those who claim to believe.

What happens when the constructed god in whom we have believed and placed our trust proves to be but a figment of our creative imagination? To whom do we turn for help? To whom or what do we turn for strength and rejuvenation? To whom shall we pray when we are threatened or faced with severe illness, tragedy, and death? To whom shall we turn when the lives of our children are threatened by forces of war, disease, pestilence, crime, unemployment, recreational drugs, and rampant sexually transmitted infections and diseases?

In short, who will bail us out of our human dilemmas? If we are not the product of a caring, loving, creator god then who made us? From whence did we come? If, on the one hand, we scoff at the idea that we are here on this earth by chance and, on the other hand, if the idea of god is no longer palpable, then how can we possibly understand who we are or from where we come? If the idea of an all-loving, all knowing, and all-powerful deity is no longer acceptable to our understanding of life then how do we understand our being?

At times Hebrew and Christian sacred literature sound so convincing and the great hymns of the church sound so powerful that we think to ourselves, in truth, all we need do is to trust and believe. Yet every time we try this we become re-committed for awhile until something comes our way that crashes us back into disillusionment and hopelessness, discouragement and despair. Our friends, like Job's three friends, counsel us to "hang-in" and "just trust" and don't ask so many unanswerable questions. If you are like me when I was in the throes of doubt and despair, you might remind yourself that you are created in the image of god and therefore you must use your god-given mind and it is no shame to doubt and question and seek eternal verities. This might tide you over until the next bout with existential doubt. One day you may stumble onto the grand insight that says your heart will never be able to accept what your mind rejects. This insight holds firm sway with me to this day.

Then there may come some sort of epiphany. There may come a time, probably when you least expect it, when seemingly out of nowhere comes a flash of insight that simply blows you away and at that instant you know in your heart that there is no more a god in the sky than there is a literal Santa-Claus. At that instant you know it is all a nicely packaged fairy tale. Perhaps, like the fable of the *Kings New Clothes*, you suddenly see the naked truth that we are all alone on this whirling planet. We have no one on whom to depend except ourselves, perhaps one or two loved ones, and, more likely, one or two of our fellow travelers.

John Spong describes the first fledgling steps we may take after we part with a personal hand-holding god. "Yes, it is frightening to think that there is no heavenly parent in the sky who will take care of us. We recall that moment in our human maturing process when we realized that we had become adults and that we, therefore, had to be responsible for ourselves. No earthly parents could protect us any longer ...The realization is dawning that we human beings are alone and therefore are responsible for ourselves, that there is no appeal to a higher power for protection. We are learning that meaning is not external to life but must be discovered in our own depths and imposed on life by an act of our own will."[1]

Your epiphany may defy all reason and sensibility. In my case it came in the face of eleven years of daily servitude as a local minister after a college degree in philosophy and a degree at Princeton Theological Seminary. In my case it was not a rebellion against my daily routine or weekly preaching. I loved to craft a sermon, rework it, revise it, and rehearse it.

My epiphany came upon me in great force and bowled me over. I recall the damning words that flowed non-stop through my wounded psyche as I concluded a grave-side funeral benediction. "Yikes! I don't believe a word of it." With me, it was all about god. I was finally strong enough to let go of god. I read god out of my life. The whole god scenario was a bad joke gone sour. One of us, either god or me, was going to die and it wasn't going to be me.

If this sounds like you, even remotely or with great variation, then I welcome you to my life and my experience as a former Presbyterian minister. I experienced all of these things. I am absolutely a skeptic and also an agnostic. As a skeptic I doubt and question. In truth, I have been a skeptic most of my life, even when I was a minister. In later years I have become a true agnostic because I believe knowledge of the ultimate is absolutely impossible. (Here I follow Immanuel Kant in his *Critique of Pure Reason*, but we will get to that much further on.)

I invite you to come with me on a journey of discovery. Mostly self-discovery. I invite you to learn from my pain and

---

1 John Shelby Spong, Why Christianity Must Change Or Die: A Bishop Speaks to Believers in Exile. San Francisco: HarperSanFrancisco, 1998. p.69.

my depression. I invite you to learn from my attempt to put my life back together without ever again turning to a constructed theistic deity.[2] I invite you to share my mid and late life adventure into the insights of both psychology and philosophy in my attempt to recover my identity and give birth to myself. I invite you to share my personal renaissance, my personal re-birth into a life that I continue to find filled with purpose, meaning, and fulfillment.

---

2 John F. Crosby, *The Flipside of Godspeak: Theism as Constructed Reality*. Eugene, Oregon: Resource *Publications*, an imprint of Wipf and Stock, 2007.

CHAPTER 1. THE LOSS OF MY GOD

It was 1966. I was walking away from the grave. As I recall that mid — November day there was a chill in the air with graying and foreboding skies. The gentleman in the coffin had been a kind man, mid-eighties, lived an honorable, if nondescript life. What was about to happen wasn't his fault. In fact, he had nothing to do with it. It just happened to be his funeral and his grave.

I had just intoned, "Now, cherishing memories that are forever sacred, sustained by a faith that is stronger than death and comforted by the hope of a life that shall endless be, we commit the body of our loved one now departed, tenderly, reverently, and lovingly, in the sure and certain hope of eternal life through our Lord Jesus Christ. Amen.

Even though I was a Presbyterian these words were not from the Presbyterian *Book of Common Worship*. They were adopted from a Congregationalist cleric with whom I had worked in my first pastoral venue, but nevertheless words that I had intoned 127 times over a period of eleven years in three different pastorates.

A crisis had been building up inside me for some time. As I look back from the vantage point of years, I think my loss of faith began on November 22, 1963. Of course I knew that Presidents Lincoln, McKinley, and Garfield had been assassinated but the death of John Kennedy caught me completely and totally off guard. I simply could not reconcile his death with the concept of a loving and caring all-powerful God. I wish that I had been able to cry. I never did. I handled his funeral and death with a stoic posture. Not that it would have mattered. JFK was still dead. To this day I think crying and verbalizing my pain (even screaming), would have helped me in my grief, perhaps by helping me to abandon my stoic refusal to question the ways of God.

After November 22, 1963, I swallowed hard and returned to the land of the living. But my pain was growing within me, much like a cancer. Silently. Steadily. Inexorably. Nonetheless, soon I forgot about JFK, at least in my everyday consciousness. Too much to attend to in the daily round of work and life.

In the spring of 1965 I started feeling pain from every direction. Marjorie and I had taken a three-day tenth anniversary wedding trip during which I felt overwhelmed with anxiety and depression. It was about this time that the sweats started. I would be sitting in a chair, having put down a book or newspaper and now doing nothing, literally nothing, and a feeling of emptiness and panic would sweep over me, leaving me in a state of hot and sweaty nervousness. At times the sweats would overwhelm me. They left me feeling bereft and vulnerable. I remember thinking I must be coming down with something.

In August there was the first of three deaths in the congregation. A young wife and mother had been released by her psychiatrist to whom I had referred her. She proudly announced to me she was discharged. "Guess what," she said with a jaunty smile on her face, "He released me." Two days later at six a.m. a phone call awakened me: She had killed herself. Overdosed! To this day I wished I had phoned the psychiatrist as soon as the lady told me she had been discharged! It probably wouldn't have changed anything but at least I could have processed the situation in the light of the psychiatrist's response.

Four months later there was the six year old who died from heart surgery. In the evening the father phoned from New York City to tell me that the lad was doing fine. When the phone rang at 3:00 a.m. I knew he was dead! I was later told that death was the result of a mistake in a medical procedure. In a day or so I found myself sitting in the parent's living room suggesting to the family that it must have been God's will.

I recall walking home late that evening. A frigid December snow was on the ground and I could hear the crunch, crunch, crunch beneath my feet. Then it happened. It dawned on my consciousness that I had suggested to these grieving parents that their son's death was God's will. At this, almost immediately, I arched over and vomited. I wretched and wretched and wretched. It was as if I had to rid myself of those terrible words I had spoken to the grieving parents. How could I have said that? Why did I cop out? What kind of thinking was going through my mind? "God's will, my foot! John, what in hell were you thinking?"

In the ensuing February of 1966 there was a sixteen-year-old who was absolutely determined to visit his girl friend in the middle of a raging three day blizzard. His dad stood at the door and forbade him to leave the safety of the house. But there was no stopping him. The trek through the woods was nigh impossible, but since when does a sixteen-year-old listen to a father's warning? This boy/man was experienced in the use of snowshoes — the kind that look like tennis rackets. Alas, after several weeks and several community sponsored searches, his dad found him sitting under a tree at the end of a hedgerow. He'd likely walked in circles in the midst the blizzard's fury. Sat down to rest. That's all there was to that. Gone forever!

By this time I was experiencing an extra heavy dose of day sweats and night sweats. It felt like a purging. There was also a symptom that caused me to feel like I was going nuts that was much milder than the sweats. This was a constant tearing in my left eye. It just never seemed to stop or let up. There were no tears per se, just the feeling of slight moistness. I was grieving and this was an archetypical tear, but how to deal with it? How to make it stop? And, of course, the sweats were a purging, but how to cope with them? How to make them stop? I believed then as I do now that symptoms are a harbinger of something gone awry. But what, precisely?

And so it was that in early '66, after the death of the lad in the blinding blizzard, I sensed that my "calling" to be a minister was in peril. I referred myself into psychotherapy. My first attempt was a washout. Perhaps more to the point, a joke! People get paid good money for this? After the therapist started talking about his relatives and something about John Calvin, even a question or two about Calvin's theology, I made tracks. Shortly thereafter I learned of a psychiatrist at the Upstate Medical Center in Syracuse. I stayed the course for about a year. Once per week. Worked my life through. I wanted to discover what forces had drawn me into the ministry. I knew my parents had carefully steered me into a church-centered life. But I was the one who made the choice to declare for the ministry. The church was the center of my childhood and youth. I always had a crush on one of the girls and all my youthful romantic fantasies were centered in the safe shelter of so-called Christian ethics and Christian morality. Even the Sunday night youth group theological-philosophical discussions and bull sessions commanded my complete attention.

But back to the gravesite. When I had walked no more than five or so feet from the grave, prior to engaging with the bereaved, an internal voice of sharp protest welled up within me. It was not a voice from without like St. Paul supposedly experienced on the road to Damascus. It was a strong and authoritative voice from within, as if one part of me was scolding and correcting another part of me. The words came pouring forth:

"I don't believe a word of it!"

That's all there was. A few simple words that would change my life forever. No drum rolls! No shouting! No antics! No bolts of lightning! No bright flashes of light! No claps of thunder! Those eight words have remained firm in my memory for over four decades and I have never been seriously tempted to repent of them. "I still do not believe a word of it."

But there was pain. Oh yes! I left the gravesite and returned home, announcing to my wife that I had had it — that I was leaving the ministry. I announced to her that I had no idea of where I would go or what I would do, but that I was getting out. Period. No more ministry. Later that evening there were tears as I phoned my liberal Presbyterian cleric father-in-law and told him I was getting out. That was the first and last time I was able to actually shed tears. There would be much grief work ahead but never again would the tears flow. Granddad, as my wife and our three sons, aged 3, 6, and 7, affectionately called him, listened to my tale of woe. He even seemed to understand my total disillusionment with the whole idea of God and humankind's dependence upon such a being. He spoke no words of reproach or "now, now, you've just had a bad day" or "you'll get over it soon enough."

Several months later Granddad did say that he thought that someday I would return. To that statement I did not offer retort. I simply let it pass, little knowing that a church of some prestige would soon invite me to apply to become a candidate in their search for a new minister. By the time that happened I had interviewed for admission to a philosophy program in a near-by college where I was told bluntly that

I would be better off staying away from philosophy and departments thereof, even though philosophy had been my undergraduate major at Denison University. And so the church still beckoned while the possibility of graduate study seemed to become a door slammed in my face. But this is to get ahead of my story.

I shared the graveside experience with my psychiatrist. I recall only his considered questions to me as to why I wished to exit the ministry. Why could I not re-adapt, re-tool, and become a different sort of cleric? Why could I not take a new me into my theological future? But I would have none of it. God and I were through with each other. I told my psychiatrist that one of us must die. Either god or me! Let it be god. I have a new life to live and I don't need my Teddy Bear god anymore.

My paid friend, as I frequently thought of my psychiatrist, had been a great help to me because as I told him my tale I was learning and internalizing a new self-sustaining autonomy. At age thirty-five I was slowly shedding my defenses and my psychological safety devices — my dependency on the god creation of my wish dreams. All the while I had been voraciously reading Rollo May, Erich Fromm, Karen Horney, Harry Stack Sullivan, Leslie Weatherhead, Viktor Frankl, Carl Rogers, Hermann Hesse, and Franz Kafka. I was growing up. I was slowly outgrowing my childish god-construct. Somewhere along the way my sweats stopped and my tearing ceased. Somewhere along the way I began to give birth to myself. This birthing was a process instead of a once-for-all event. It is a process that continues even today in the matrix of new experiences and new challenges. Today I look upon the birthing process as my never ending renaissance.

But back to the gravesite. In the short run, Sunday was but two days hence. What was I to do? I had completed my sermon. So what? I would re-write it. A day and two nights of contemplation left me with the following plan of action.

Perhaps contrary to how others might choose to handle the situation, I determined that the problem was mine, not members of the congregation. I was not going to cry on their shoulders or use them in any conscious way to work through my dilemma. I further determined that I would not lay my trip upon them in the near and foreseeable future. With some changes in my theological slant I carried through a pulpit program which would do two things: It would preserve my own integrity about my transformed theological stance and it would become more pragmatic and humanistic, emphasizing the would-be Christian response to the great issues of life as well as addressing the everyday problems and choices associated with responsible daily living. Perhaps some in the congregation of several hundred would detect my revised pulpit position. Perhaps not! Regardless, I knew I was not fooling myself. My resolve to find a new way of life and being grew steadily.

As I continued to tell my tale to the psychiatrist more and more memories came to the fore. I had luxuriated in my philosophy classes at Denison where I invariably felt the urge to play devil's advocate in the discussions of free will versus determinism, transcendence versus immanence, grace versus good works, nature versus nurture, and subjective idealism versus objective realism. Such modern points of concern about the virgin birth of Jesus and the actual date of his birth, the beliefs held by fundamentalists and some conservatives and evangelicals about the inerrancy and literalism of interpretation of the scriptures never bothered me or even interested me. I never took these things seriously. Nor did I have any truck with the belief in the physical resurrection of Jesus or his alleged ascension. I had no wish to peach about the so-called miracles.[3] I had always accepted the necessity

---

3 For further information on this and related topics please see *The Flipside of Godspeak: Theism As Constructed Reality*, Appendix One, "Confession of An Apostate". Eugene, Oregon: Wipf and Stock, 2007.

of abortion and had long held to an ethic of thoroughgoing sex education as being a necessary social intervention. This was also the time I tried to master the British empiricists, Locke, Berkeley, and Hume, as they were challenged by the great Immanuel Kant and his (failed) attempt to prove the existence of god by pure reason.

Somewhere in the course of my therapy I recall feeling chagrined at telling the psychiatrist that I had been accepted at both Union theological Seminary in New York City and Princeton Theological in Princeton, N.J. I am still embarrassed that I was so naïve about theological nuances! How was I to have known that Princeton was a bastion of reformed theology and conservative in points of doctrine? Yes, I never should have gone to Princeton. I perhaps should have known better but life happens and there I was. Unfortunately, and to my detriment, another part of me soaked it all in. Perhaps it was the pietistic thread that had run through me all during my youth and late adolescence, even while I was at Denison. I had made a personal friend of God the father and God the son and slowly but surely I had internalized and then constructed a relationship best described by St. Paul, "For me to live is Christ, and to die is gain." (Philippians 1:21) and "It is no longer I who live, but Christ who lives in me." (Galatians 2:20). At any rate, for better or for worse, I shared with my therapist everything that came to my mind. No holds barred.

I liked the theology of Paul Tillich and the theological disciplines of the higher and lower criticism. I tried to be thorough in my exegesis of scripture using the Greek and Hebrew texts. Slowly I grew into a new frame of mind. After all, if there is no god then why bother? The historical Jesus still interested me but beyond that I increasingly felt it was all much ado about nothing!

I shared with my wife and my psychiatrist my evolving plans. I would go back to school, preferably Syracuse University, and enroll in a graduate program, most likely in some form of counseling or in clinical psychology. In my three pastoral venues I had always been involved in heavy doses of marriage and family counseling situations and had long felt ill equipped and under-qualified for this work. A graduate program along these lines would be most welcome. Within three months I had been accepted as a doctoral student in the *Department of Family Relations and Child Development* at Syracuse University. Concomitant with this degree program I would be able to submit myself to clinical supervision in the *American Association for Marriage and Family Therapy* (AAMFT).

Of course there came a time when I would have to part with my psychiatrist who by now had become a pseudo father figure whom I both respected and genuinely liked. Just as I had been scared and frightened when I quit praying to the god I had once believed in (What would happen when I quit praying? Would the world stop? Would I die of a heart attack or a stroke?), I also had some misgivings about breaking with my therapist. Would I be able to walk alone? Was I ready to go solo? What if I were to stumble or fall down? No matter! Pick yourself up and get on with your life. Sheldon Kopp had it right when he said:

The psychotherapy patient must also come to this heavy piece of understanding, that he does *not* need the therapist. The most important things that each man (sic) must learn, no one else can teach him. Once he accepts this disappointment, he will be able to stop depending on the therapist, the guru who turns out to be just another struggling human being. Illusions die hard, and it is painful to yield to the insight that a grown-up can be no man's disciple. This discovery does not mark the end of the search, but a new beginning." [4]

After three years of graduate school I completed my doctorate at Syracuse and my clinical training for AAMFT. Dur-

---

4 Sheldon B. Kopp, *If You Meet the Buddha on The Road, Kill Him: The Pilgrimage of Psychotherapy Patients.* Palo Alto, CA. Science and Behavior Books.1972 . Bantam Edition.) p.56.

ing this time I also met with a committee from the Presbytery of Cayuga-Syracuse to process my request to demit the ministry. Since this was of my own choosing it really wasn't quite the same as defrocking but in the end it amounts to the same thing.

On April 7, 1970, Presbytery met in a beautiful edifice at the northern end of one of New York State's heralded Finger Lakes. The committee that had been meeting with me thought it best that I not speak to the Presbytery. (After all, the Presbytery should be spared the details of my blasphemous and heretical views.) I agreed with this inasmuch as I would have needed a good twelve to fifteen minutes if I were to speak. When the appointed time came I stood before the Presbytery. The clerk read the motion stating that John Crosby, the petitioner, had requested the dissolution of the relationship between himself and the Presbytery. The moderator started to ask for a vote when a friend of mine in the rear of the sanctuary rose to a point of order. He announced that he would not vote on such a motion until he heard from John. At this the moderator banged his gavel and told me I could speak for no more than five minutes.

What to say in five minutes? I recall the first thing I said was that the older I got the less certain I was of anything having to do with god or ultimate reality. (I was 38 at the time.) I said I did not belong in the pulpit and that I wished to be relieved of my ordination vows. I no longer believed in the trinity of God the Father, God the Son, and God the Holy Spirit. I no longer accepted the Bible as "the word of God, the only infallible rule of faith and practice." And I no longer "sincerely receive and adopt the Confession of Faith of this Church, as containing the system of doctrine taught in the Holy Scriptures." (i.e., The Westminster Confession of Faith.)[5] I also said that Paul Tillich's reference to the "god beyond the god

---

5 *The Book of Common Worship*, 1946. The Presbyterian Church in the United States of America.

of theism" was the only conjectural possibility about god that I could even remotely consider.[6]

When I finished the moderator called for a vote. Unanimous. I took my final journey down the center aisle. I must have looked forlorn, sad, and down-in-the-mouth, but to make the assumption that my body language was indicative of my inner feelings would have been to make a false judgment. This is because even as I walked down the aisle I was smiling inside myself. I was rejoicing that I was free. No more holy orders! No more reverend stuff! No more hypocrisy. Several of my friends met me in the vestibule to greet me and say good-by. One in particular said he envied my courage. Another commented that "lots of guys won't sleep very well tonight." Since that time I have come to realize that many more men would leave behind their "holy orders" were it not for the financial reality of being set adrift in a world for which they were unprepared.

May fourth, 1970—the terrible Kent State University killings. My dissertation defense was scheduled at an off-campus site just in case Syracuse University became violent. Thanks to a great job by the Chief-of-Police of the city of Syracuse this show of violence never happened.

In June Marjorie, our three boys, and I made the trek to Bloomington, Indiana, where I was to begin my new career. By now, however, we were so poor that I felt it necessary to cash in my pension. The Presbyterian Board of Pensions redeemed the three per cent per pay check that I had invested, but in order to receive this I had to sign off on the ten per cent per month the church had contributed in my behalf to the Board of Pensions as part of my salary. We had invested in the pension fund for nine of our eleven years of ministry. When I turned 65 I made several inquiries about my prospects for suing the Presbyterian Board of Pensions for the

---

6 Paul Tillich. *The Courage To Be*. New Haven: The Yale University Press. 1952. Chapter Six.

withheld ten per cent plus accumulated interest. After all, I had signed under duress. It was rightfully my money. I had earned it. "Forget it," the attorneys said. 1970 was pre ERISA and I did not stand a chance of winning. And if per chance I did win, the attorney fees and costs would be far greater than the settlement. Those Presbyterians had me by the tail and wouldn't let go!

Here ends my tale of loss. But nothing in the loss could possibly detract from the peace, satisfaction, and fulfillment that my renaissance would bring.

In truth, the death of my personal god helped me grow up. In the chapters that follow I shall attempt to draw as clear a picture as I can of the various steps and hurdles that I went through as I attempted to reconstruct my life. I will share with you, the reader, the focal points of my journey and the various challenges to my thought processes. Some of this work I did before I entered therapy, some during my year of therapy, and some even as long as twenty to thirty years later, as I became exposed to later researchers and later theorists, especially as a clinician in marriage and family therapy.

I hold out to the reader the stages and steps of my journey simply as pointers to what I think is necessary for personal re-birth. Everyone's personal journey will be different. Certainly we need to come into direct confrontation with our own non-being, as Paul Tillich describes it. We also need to be aware, in my opinion, of the role that anxiety and stress, both negative and positive, play in our lives. I believe the role that loss plays in our lives is crucial and that how we cope with loss goes a long way toward our becoming who we are and how we survive. We need to be aware of the importance of courage, "...not as the absence of fear, but the ability to carry on with dignity in spite of it."[7]

---

[7] Scott Turow, *The Burden of Proof*. New York: Farrar, Giroux, and Straus, 1990. Chapter 47

In all of this I think it is important to dig into the literature on the "self." In doing so we need to be especially aware of the role and power of our belief system because, in my view, these beliefs undergird the gradual development of our life-long thematic "constructs" that form the infrastructure upon which we build everything else, especially the values that lace our life and give rise to meaning and purpose. Perhaps the most common question posed to me was the question of being good without god (Chapter Nine).

If the reader gives herself or himself to the concepts, thoughts, and categories of these pages there will likely be a gradual evolution from god-dependency to self-dependency. There will likely be a renaissance experience of survival and re-birth second to no religious or spiritual practice known to humankind.

Chapter 2. The Primal Fear

What does my tale of loss have to do with you? Was there something about the subtitle that caught your eye? Or perhaps this book came to you as a gift. Where are you on the question of God?

I am concerned with the task of picking up the pieces after faith in god has somehow fizzled out. My purpose in writing is to provide guidelines and building blocks as you reconstruct your life without reference to a deity.

I have several questions I would like to pose before we wade into these issues any further.

1. How did it come to be that you believed in god in the first place?

2. Describe the god you used to believe in.

3. Did you believe in some sort of eternal punishment?

4. Describe any memories you may have had related to fear of death.

5. Did you think you wanted to live again after this life and perhaps forever?

6. In what way did you believe that life after death gave meaning to your existence?

7. Do you still believe that it is god who is the basis of your moral good behavior and that without god you would be immoral?

8. If there were no god, what would you now be doing differently in your daily living?

9. What did you gain by your former attachment to god?

Have you read *The End of Faith* by Sam Harris? Or *The God Delusion* by Richard Dawkins, *god is not Great* by Christopher Hitchens, or *Godless*, by Dan Barker? The book you are holding now begins where those books leave off. As good as they are, they hardly begin to fill the void of godlessness that perhaps you are facing in the reality of your everyday life.

The Functions and Purpose of Religion

Religion has been defined, and continues to this day to be defined, in many and diverse ways. Just as there are countless varieties of religious experiences there are countless varieties of religions. There is theism and deism, monotheism and polytheism, spiritualism, asceticism, and all manner of idol worship including baal worship and religions of the earth such as paganism. Just as there is a vast literature dealing with the history of religion and religious development there is also a considerable literature on the development of the idea of god.[8] The history of religion and the history of god-thought are not necessarily the same but they do share a parallel history.

In view of this, it is important to ask what is the chief purpose of religion? Since there are many and varied kinds and types of religions it is important that we differentiate between them. We must ask what role or roles does it ful-

---

8 Karen Armstrong. *A History of God*. New York: Alfred A. Knopf. 1994.

fill? What needs does it meet? What are its functions? Is it possible to pinpoint an overriding chief function or purpose? Again, the answer depends on which religion or belief system we are considering. Buddhism and Hinduism may yield far divergent functions than Shintoism or Confucianism. By way of general answer, there are many functions religion fulfills including the philosophical function, the sociological function, the psychological function, the cultural function, and even the political function. The ancient philosopher Seneca is reputed to have said: "Religion is regarded by the common people as true, by the wise as false, by the rulers as useful."

Revealed and Natural Theology

In the chapters that follow we will be addressing the basic monotheism of the three traditions of faith that evolved from the patriarch Abraham (born circa 1996 BCE[9]). Most specifically, we will concern ourselves with the theistic beliefs, tenets of faith, creeds, and dogma of various Christian persuasions including Roman Catholicism, traditional mainline Protestantism including the Reformed and Confessing traditions, evangelical Protestantism, Fundamentalists, Pentecostals, Holiness associations, and the Mormons. There are also the Quakers, Mennonites, and Amish. These groups, whether liberal or conservative, are strongly theistic in the theological tradition of what is known as "revealed" theology. Theism implies that god is a transcendent god extending throughout the universe as well as an immanent god who is present with humans in all their endeavors, experiences, and tragedies and is solicitous of a personal relationship with human beings via personal service, prayer, and the commitment of personal trust and devotion.

---

9 *The New Westminster Dictionary of the Bible.* Henry Snyder Gehman, Philadelphia: The Westminster Press, 1970. p. 165.

In the United States today, a strong nationalistic and pietistic version of an immanent god is promoted, one who demands a type of patriotic allegiance. This version of theism thrives on the idea of god as a national plenipotentiary who will save our nation from the ravages of totalitarianism, rampant liberalism, rampant conservatism, materialism, fascism, and socialism of any stripe or description.

Revealed religion and revealed theology are based on authority stemming from the top downward, i.e., some great god event revealing itself to humankind. Even though the supernatural deity is transcendent it is also immanent in that it involves itself in the history of human affairs and the everyday problems, joys, and tragedies of human existence. Revealed religion always posits a supreme transcendent and supernatural authority to which the celebrant is expected to be obedient and submissive. Revealed religion is motivated by the human attempt to somehow transcend the bounds of mortal existence in obedience to the supreme authority and author of creation. When obedience is achieved, the celebrant is assured that some form of eternal life where reunion with loved ones from prior ages may be accomplished.

Contrary to revealed theology and revealed religion, natural theology and natural religion have their roots in humankind's observation and experience of the micro-universe and the macro-universe. Natural religion and natural theology attempt to base belief upon human reasoning and alleged logic.[10] It reasons from the bottom up, i.e., makes assumptions based on what we observe and experience about the natural order to a higher order reality. Not all, but certainly the great majority of people who accept some sort of natural theology are also those who find in religious belief an affinity with the

---

10 William Paley. Natural Theology: Or Evidences of the Existence and Attributes of the Deity, Collected from the Appearances of Nature. Boston: 1802. (Gould and Lincoln, 1860 Edition).

sense of awe and wonder, of splendor and majesty, of humility and grand identification with all the natural forces of the universe. Folks who adhere to religion based on natural theology rarely participate in prayers of repentance, confession, and personal petition (the "give me, god" blues), that are common to those who accept revealed theology with its emphasis on personal piety.

While there are other distinctions between revealed and natural theology, the key difference is the question of authority. Natural religion and theology does not require appealing to a powerful authority figure as does revealed religion and authority. Natural theology has rarely, if ever, motivated people to kill one another, to wage wars and crusades, or to punish and torture those who have demonstrated disobedience. Revealed theology almost always looks to law-givers and commandment-givers, to authorities who must be obeyed and to institutions that claim to carry out the will of the saints, sages, potentates, priests, bishops, cardinals, pastors, and ministers.

Is Death the End of Life?

There are several seminal books that must be considered in addressing the question of God and Life beyond death. One such book, a Pulitzer Prize winner, was written by Ernest Becker, *The Denial of Death*.[11] While the vast majority of human beings come to learn the fact of the inevitability and finality of physiological death, it is not necessarily true that all persons accept this fact at face value. Humans are quite clever and ingenious in their methods of denial and escape from the biological and physiological condition known as rigor mortis. I once talked with a gentleman who had read Becker's work (he said: "quite thoroughly") and he assured me that while Becker was correct about the denial of death, he (Becker) was

---

11 Ernest Becker. *The Denial of Death.* New York: The Free Press. 1973.

talking about physical death as opposed to spiritual death! This gentleman's statement, of course, only goes to confirm and validate what Becker is talking about. By spiritualizing the fact of death we do, in truth, deny it! Becker's work stands as one of the seminal efforts to illustrate and explain how psychological repression serves to protect us from the reality and finality of death as the final chapter for each of us.

A second seminal book is *The Future of An Illusion* by Sigmund Freud.[12] A third is *Escape From Freedom* by Erich Fromm.[13] A fourth is *The Courage To Be*, by Paul Tillich.[14] Of course there are many others to which I will be referring in due course. For now, let me simply say that I believe the *fear of death is the chief motivational factor of all religions in the tradition of revealed theology*. To a far lesser extent, the fear of death may also be a key motivational factor in the tradition of natural theology. The difference is that in traditions stemming from revealed theology the emphasis is on some sort of salvation and immortality extending into a future life. In the traditions stemming from natural theology the emphasis is on a melding or blending into the stream of matter, time, and eternity, i.e., a merging into transcendence with an elan or force. Forrest Church, a Unitarian, is representative of the tradition of natural theology when he says "Religion is our human response to the dual reality of being alive and having to die."[15]

The Crisis of Faith

In the pages and chapters that follow my central concern is with folks who have come to the point where they no longer believe in the theistic god of their childhood and youth, indeed maybe even the god of their middle adulthood and old

---

12 Sigmund Freud. *The Future Of An Illusion.* Vienna, *Die Zukunft einer Illusion*, Liveright Publishing Corp. 1927. (Revised Anchor Book Edition: 1964)

13 Erich Fromm. *Escape From Freedom.* New York: Holt, Rinehart,& Winston.1941.

14 Paul Tillich. *The Courage To Be.* New Haven: Yale University Press 1952.

15 Forrest Church. *Love & Death.* Boston: Beacon Press. 2008. p. X, Intro..

age. As a result of this loss of faith, many people feel a deep personal loss. They feel bereft, perhaps as one adrift on an iceberg or in a lifeboat, floating about here and there without chart and compass. Some of these millions wish to construct a new faith for themselves based on human reason. Others turn (or return) to a life of contented solitude even though they feel an inner emptiness. Still others, perhaps the majority of those who have experienced a crisis of faith, feel lost and alone, uncertain and unsure of what they presently believe. Many of these have rejected the easy answers of theism but they remain in a state of uncertainty mixed with anxious confusion.

The reason for the feeling of dis-ease and even bewilderment is the unspoken fear of nothingness. For some this is the abyss or the void. If there is no god, then what? Is there no possibility for meaning and purpose in life? Is it all a joke? When faith is lost to whom does one turn? When belief is riddled with doubt and skepticism what authority should one embrace? If the idea of god is an invention of the human mind as we humans attempt to make sense out of life, then does this not mean that all life is relative and all answers tentative? Does this not mean that there is no ultimate source of authority because there is not any evidence supporting such authority?

What most of us fail to understand is that we have been conditioned, programmed if you will, to believe that god gives meaning and purpose to life and that without god all is lost and meaningless. This programming has been (and still is) very subtle and very powerful. It has been thrust at us via family, neighborhood, elementary and secondary school, Boy Scouts, Girl Scouts, Future Farmers of America, preachers, Sunday schools, churches, temples, mosques, synagogues, and politicians of all stripes. At the heart of this popular theistic theology is the belief in a life beyond this one. Whether it is called immortality, eternal life, salvation, the elect, or Sheol, (the place of the dead), the belief is subtle and commanding, promised and guaranteed by the supreme authority as being absolutely true and trustworthy. What we further fail to see or understand is that if we deny or otherwise reject the god who offers us the life beyond this life, we will not only be shutting ourselves off from a future paradise of life with god, we may also be letting ourselves in for an eternity of torture and the hellfire of damnation.

Thus, the subtle message is that to abandon faith in god is to open oneself up to the possibility of damnation for all eternity. When this message is thoroughly internalized and constantly reinforced it results in the supreme motivation to remain a believer. In short, the only way to avoid death is to believe. An excellent modern day description of how preachers, especially evangelical and fundamentalist clerics, use the art of preaching to stir up their congregations into a state of fear and anxiety is in the book *godless* by Dan Barker.[16] Historic descriptions of the creation of fear and anxiety include John Milton's *Paradise Lost*, Dante's *Divine Comedy*, and John Bunyan's *The Pilgrims Progress*.[17] One may also turn on the radio or television at almost any time of day to hear hellfire preaching with all the accoutrements, including threat, shame, ridicule, condemnation, humiliation, and fright,

One may also witness the popularity of an American nationalistic religion which seems to assume that when national heroes, singers, actors, athletes, and other social and political legends die, they will be in a special place where they can look down upon earthlings with either pride or shame, depending on recent national events. In sports we have become accustomed to baseball batters crossing themselves before they take their stance at the plate. We are treated to football players, quarterbacks and receivers, kneeling in an attitude of

---

16Dan Barker, op. cit. Especially see the four chapters in Part I

17John Milton, *Paradise Lost*, 1674; Dante, *The Divine Comedy*, 1321; John Bunyan, *The Pilgrim's Progress*, 1678 & 1684.

prayer after catching the pass and/or side-stepping would-be tacklers as they cross the goal line.

Belief in Afterlife

By and large the greatest motivation in theistic belief is deliverance from death via some sort of salvation or after-life. The primal fear underlying the professed beliefs of the Christian persuasions is the fear of death. Although often repressed and denied, the chief function of theistic belief is to enable humankind to cope with the inevitability of death. Becker says "...the final terror of self-consciousness is the knowledge of one's own death..." [18] This primal fear underlies the lives of most of us, as far as I can tell. For some mortals, the primal fear is so unbearable that the escape is suicide, a total embracing of the very thing that is feared the most. For others the terror leads to some form of mental illness, a psychosis that protects the subject from perceived reality. For still others it is a blunting, restricting, and narrowing down of perceived reality via neurosis.[19] For many devout Christians, it is as though they were sharing their earthly pilgrimage with the Apostle Paul who asks: "Wretched man that I am! Who will deliver me from this body of death?" (Romans 7:24)

---

18 Becker, op. cit. p. 70.

19 *The Oxford Dictionary of Psychology*, Andrew M. Coleman. Oxford: Oxford University Press, 2001. "From Greek *neuron* a nerve + *osis* indicating a process or state. ... The word was coined in 1777 by the Scottish physician William Cullen. An imprecise term for a relatively mild mental disorder with predominantly distressing symptoms and without loss of insight or reality testing, and without apparent organic etiology, including anxiety neurosis...depersonalization neurosis... depressive neurosis...hysterical neurosis...obsessive compulsive neurosis...and phobic neurosis." In common usage this word often begs for precise definition. As Erich Fromm points out, the so-called well-adjusted person may, in fact, be neurotic while the "neurotic person can be characterized as somebody who was not ready to surrender completely in the battle for his self...If we differentiate the two concepts of normal and neurotic, we come to the following conclusion: the person who is normal in terms of being well adapted is often less healthy than the neurotic person in terms of human values." Erich Fromm, 1941. *Escape From Freedom*. Op. cit. (Chapter Five, Mechanisms of Escape.)

For many others, the fear of death is consciously dealt with via the use of drugs, narcotics, spirits, and opiates of varying descriptions. Further, on the level of the conscious, there is the use of denial, avoidance, and the deliberate use of suppression. On the level of the unconscious there is the tranquilizing effect of defense mechanisms, safety devices, and escape mechanisms whereby we bind the ill effects of anxiety so as to enable us to face the everyday burdens and challenges of perceived reality. And, as Becker points out so well in his classic work, *The Denial of Death*, there is repression.[20] In a frontal assault on Freud, Becker states: "*Consciousness of death* is the primary repression, not sexuality."[21] Repression is probably the most powerful of all psychic phenomena. It is unconscious and it fills the function of protecting us from our most horrendous fears and related anxieties.

A Personal Note

Perhaps the reader is now wondering just how all this business of fear of death applies to her or him. After all, few of us go about our daily lives carrying this primal fear on our shoulder. We suppress it. We push it down—deep inside. We deny it. We coat it with euphemisms. We express our deepest and most heart-felt regrets and sympathies to friends who are facing their own death, or a death in their family, while deep within our inner self we are relieved that it is not we who are dying.

"But is this wrong?" you may ask. Not at all! I am simply trying to illustrate how subtle the denial of death is and how we conspire within our own inner self to blunt the cutting edge of its inevitability. Again, you may ask, "What would you have us do? Surely we are not encouraged to be morbid and forlorn, full of depression and melancholy?" "Surely we

---

20 Becker, op. cit., p. 70.
21 Becker, op. cit., p. 96.

are not to be zombies or automatons who are afraid of our shadow? Surely we are not to be afraid of life in order to be fully cognizant of our own demise?" You would be absolutely correct in protesting in this vein. But we may well ask: At what point do we live fully and enthusiastically without at the same time engaging in some sort of denial of our personal demise? In other words, at what point can we both embrace the truth of our demise while embracing the fullness, joy, and wonder of our existence?

My purpose is to help the reader grasp the truth that the more we arm ourselves against the reality of death, the more we are reduced in life. The greater our fear of nothingness, the less we give purpose and meaning to our own lives, to our endeavors, to our ambitions, and to our various daily pursuits. Millions of honest and morally upright persons are reluctant to break with their idea of god because of their suppressed and repressed fear of death. As long as their conscious and unconscious defenses work, as we have discussed in this chapter, these "believers" will likely continue to believe in some form of afterlife which will protect them from the stark, naked truth that death is absolute and final and admits of no exceptions or rationalizations. Death does admit of spiritualization but this is nothing except another form of denial. The more we spiritualize it, the more we protect ourselves against the naked truth that with our own demise we no longer have consciousness of any kind or description.

What I have come to realize is that, for me, if a belief cannot be factually substantiated, that is, if a belief cannot be reasonably demonstrated to be true, valid, and authentic, then it can be of no personal comfort or strength. I think Christopher Hitchens had it right when he said that, "...extraordinary claims require extraordinary evidence and what can be asserted without evidence can also be dismissed without evidence."[22]

---

22 Christopher Hitchens. "Mommie Dearest," *Slate*, Oct. 20, 2003. ‹Slate.msn.com.›

After god dies, I personally see only two possible avenues to immortality. The first is my hope that my mate and my sons and their families will nourish a remembrance of me throughout their life span, i.e., that I will continue to live on in their memory. Hopefully, also, one or several grandchildren will keep me in their memories, as well as a few close friends and former students. This avenue to immortality, as I see it, is not a hope but a fact: "Nature conquers death not by creating eternal organisms but by making it possible for ephemeral ones to procreate."[23] Is it not enough that the natural forces of our universe and our planet have evolved in a way that insures our continued existence in and through the lives of our offspring? Is it not enough that you began life as a zygote, one sperm out of millions having fertilized your mother's ovum, and that you have somehow survived to this point? You hope to continue to live and flourish for years to come. Yet you know very well in your inner mind that there comes an end to all things and this end is nothing to fear because it is the natural conclusion to life.

A second possible avenue to immortality is through the accumulated grand product of our life efforts, and, even if we have no offspring or descendents, the memories we leave with other people who have known us. This form of immortality is defined by what we leave behind. It is what we bequeath to future generations. We create, we build, we attempt to make this world a better place. We seek to create works that will make a difference to future generations. We legislate documents of justice including court decisions as well as codes of law for the smallest towns and villages. Our participation in shaping and maintaining the social order is, or can be, a means for individual citizens to feel that they have made some contribution.

We seek to obtain and share knowledge and create avenues to aesthetic pleasure, through education, architecture,

---

23 Becker, op. cit., p. 163.

art, painting, music of all types and varieties, literature of all descriptions, drama, fiction, biography, history, diaries, expeditions, explorations, and research within and outside of academic institutions. Forms of volunteer service, be it as a volunteer fire fighter or a volunteer in the local hospital or running for and serving on school boards and local town/city councils and committees — these are contributions to the welfare of all of us, whether our actual name is remembered or not. All the efforts of our minds and all we do to further the hopes and possibilities of future generations contribute to the enrichment of the human race. This is the platform upon which future generations will build. This is what people mean by paying forward. All of this is a form of immortality which gives meaning and purpose to our own existence as well as to the lives of others.

And yet, even though it is the natural and logical conclusion to life, it remains our primal fear. In truth, it remains our primal fear until we have the personal courage to face it head on without encumbrances and fairytales and the threatening doomsday scenarios of theologians, seers, and would-be prophets.

CHAPTER 3. THE ANXIETY OF EXISTENCE

Paul Tillich, in his famous work, *The Courage To Be*, says, "The fear of death determines the element of *anxiety* in every fear...The basic anxiety, the anxiety of a finite being about the threat of nonbeing, cannot be eliminated. It belongs to existence itself."[24] Thus we see that the primal fear of death underlies humankind's most basic anxiety, the anxiety of existence.

The subject of anxiety is not an easy one.[25] I shall attempt to do a bird's eye view of this subject so as to help the reader see as clearly as possible what he or she will need to do to carve out a new everyday existence without the anxiety that often comes with loss,— in this case, the loss of faith in god. In order to do this we first need to clarify some basics about the psychology of anxiety. First, there is a simple formula that enjoys widespread acceptance in the wake of the professional work of several very well known psychologists and psychoanalysts. Freud's first theory of anxiety stipulated that

---

24 Tillich, op. cit. pp.38- 39.
25 John F. Crosby. "Theories of Anxiety: A Theoretical Perspective." *The American Journal of Psychoanalysis* 36:237-248. 1976.

repression caused anxiety.[26] This proved to be quite wrong. It is the other way around: *Anxiety causes repression.* Freud, in his second theory of anxiety, also came to embrace this formula. Karen Horney [27] and Rollo May[28] have clarified this formula and demonstrated its validity quite beyond doubt.

What does this mean? It means that when anxiety becomes too great to bear, our unconscious self represses it. This is the foundation for the basic belief, as elaborated by Horney, May, and Becker, that repression is not our enemy. Rather, repression comes to us as a friend to protect us against the unbearable. Repression is the prime mechanism of defense and escape. It allows us to function in the midst of disarray, guilt, shame, confusion, tragedy, pain, sorrow, grief, and death.

Fear is Not Anxiety: Anxiety is Not Fear

In the last chapter we saw that death is the primal fear. It is the fear of death that ultimately impels us into anxiety. We need to be clear that fear and anxiety are not the same thing. Fear has a specific object and it is of two kinds. Rational fear is a fear that most thoughtful people would agree upon. I have a fear of becoming ill with cancer. I fear becoming old and infirm and becoming incontinent. I fear warfare. I fear dictators. I fear fascism. As far as rational fear is concerned, we simply could not live and function if we failed to have a healthy respect for what can harm us and cause us pain and grief. Rational fear serves to keep us safe and whole and alive.

An irrational fear is quite simply a fear without reason, or, at least, without apparent reason. This could be anything from a fear that my well-tuned automobile will stall as I cross the railroad tracks to a fear that you will not like me if I tell

26 Sigmund Freud. *The Problem of Anxiety,*1936. p 111, 22. Also: *The new Introductory Lectures,* 1933, p. 86.
27 Karen Horney. *The Neurotic Personality of Our Time.* New York: W. W. Norton. p. 63, 66. 1939, *New Ways In Psychoanalysis.* New York: W. W. Norton, 1937. p. 195.
28 Rollo May. *The Meaning of Anxiety.* New York: The Ronald Press, 1950. p. 194.

you what I'm really thinking. It is a fear that I will turn into a pumpkin at midnight. It is a fear that if I wash my hair every day, I will lose it. One of the tasks of parenting is in helping a child learn and understand the difference between goblins hiding in the closet and children running into the street to retrieve a ball. Or the difference between being afraid of the dark and being fearful and afraid of animals that may be rabid.

Anxiety, on the other hand, usually does *not* have a specific object but rather is a vague feeling of dis-ease and unease, a feeling of discomfort and even a mild delirium. This is why so many people cannot pinpoint the reason for their anxiety. Anxiety is often a free-floating feeling that is well disguised simply because it doesn't directly relate to an object, event, or person. Anxiety is a big, oblong blur. It can be like a cloud of mist. It can be an internal feeling of nausea mixed with vertigo. Oftentimes free-floating anxiety can attach itself to ongoing activities and events, even sexual longing and desire. Karen Horney maintains that "just as all is not gold that glitters, so all is not sexuality that looks like it."[29] While many of our activities and pursuits are anxiety driven, it is usually extremely difficult to determine accurately just what we are anxious about. The chances are that if you can immediately pinpoint what it is that you are anxious about, you probably are suffering from a fear or phobia of some kind.

Anxiety must also be differentiated from stress. They are certainly related, but they are not the same. Like fear, stress and stressors can usually be identified. And just as we may develop great anxiety about our own mortality which will end in death, we also may develop anxiety over the various strains of stress we face in our daily lives.

In contrast to normal anxiety, neurotic anxiety is a clinical term usually reserved for neurotic anxiety disorders such as

---

29 Horney, op. cit., p. 157-159.

phobias, obsessions, and compulsions.[30] In our present consideration of the anxiety of existence, true neurotic anxiety, the psychoneuroses, are not our main concern. These neuroses are often referred to as "clinical" neuroses because they are the result of direct observation of a patient or client i.e., diagnosed and treated by clinicians. Like much of what we label as mental or emotional illness, the clinical examples are usually an exaggerated or extended form of the normal.

Angst der Kreatur

There is another kind of normal anxiety which I would label as the anxiety of existence. Others would call it an *existential* anxiety. It refers to the anxiety that, so far as we know, only human beings can experience because it is only human beings who can ponder their own existence. Karen Horney has labeled this anxiety as *angst der kreatur*. "What the phrase expresses is that factually all of us are helpless toward forces more powerful than ourselves, such as death, illness, old age, catastrophes of nature, political events, accidents. The first time we recognize this is in the helplessness of childhood, but the knowledge remains with us for our entire life. This anxiety of the *Kreatur* has in common with the basic anxiety the element of the helplessness toward greater powers, but it does not connote hostility on the part of those powers."[31]

The Anxiety of Existence

Ernst Becker goes even further than Horney. "Anxiety is the result of the perception of the truth of one's condition. What does it mean to be a *self-conscious animal*? The idea is ludicrous, if it is not monstrous. It means to know that one is food for worms. This is the terror: to have emerged from noth-

---

30 John F. Crosby. "Theories of Anxiety: A Theoretical Perspective." *The American Journal of Psychoanalysis*. 1976. 36: 237-248.
31 Horney, op. cit., p. 81.

ing, to have a name, consciousness of self, deep inner feelings, and excruciating inner yearning for life and self-expression— and with all this yet to die."[32]

Following Becker's thought — have you ever wondered about having gone through kindergarten, twelve years of school, perhaps four years of college, maybe additional post-graduate work, an apprenticeship, thirty five or forty years on the postal route or on the assembly line, a lifetime commitment in the secretarial pool, years of on-the-job training — only to be turned out to pasture at age 65 or 70 and to have little to look forward to except declining health? Perhaps Alzheimer's disease? Perhaps loss of mobility? Need I continue? And this is to say nothing of developmentally slow children, crippled children, birth defects, and offspring who will never be able to lead a normal life. Of course it was not a waste for you to have prepared and worked as you did, but this kind of thought is peculiar only to the human species.

Binding Anxiety

I don't know about you, but I have always tried to keep my anxiety of existence at a minimum. I therefore learned to "bind" my anxiety. Of course I did not know the meaning of the term, "to bind," as we are using it here. What does this binding really mean? To *bind anxiety* is to find ways and means of controlling your life so that you are minimally bothered by unwelcome thoughts, difficult problems, and unhappy anticipations. The greater our ability to bind our anxiety the more comfortable we are.

We must be very aware that anything — absolutely anything — can bind anxiety. It isn't just the activity in itself, the pursuit, the investment of energy, or the belief that is the hallmark of the "binding," but also the frequency, the quantity, the intensity, the preoccupation, the amount of time

---

32 Becker, op. cit., p. 87.

involved, and the ego investment involved. Another way of looking at the binding of anxiety is to consider how the individual integrates his or her anxiety into their life structures, processes, and relationships.

Paul Tillich shows us how our participation in various enterprises and endeavors can bind our anxiety. "The anxiety which, in its different forms, is potentially present in every individual becomes general if the accustomed structures of meaning, power, belief, and order disintegrate. These structures, as long as they are in force, keep anxiety bound within a protective system of courage by participation. The individual who participates in the institutions and ways of life of such a system is not liberated from his personal anxieties but he has means of overcoming them with well-known methods. In periods of great changes, these methods no longer work."[33] Consider how participation in religious functions and institutions serve to bind our anxiety. Consider how participation in recreational teams, sports functions, and gaming events serve to help us keep our mind off more serious and possibly threatening issues. Consider the comfort many people experience from sacerdotal ceremonies including weddings, baptisms, funerals, memorial services, and celebrations of all kinds and descriptions, including national holidays and rituals.

Michael Kerr and Murray Bowen say, "There are numerous manifestations of anxiety within an individual, each manifestation reflecting a specific way that anxiety has been 'bound.' Relationships are by far the most effective anxiety binders."[34] Many bind their anxiety by becoming over controlling of all those little things that go to make up a normal day, from the austere housekeeping, vacuuming, and dusting to the arranging of furniture, books, magazines, shoes, clothing, and clut-

---

33 Tillich, op. cit., p. 62.
34 Michael Kerr and Murray Bowen, *Family Evaluation.* New York: W. W. Norton & Company, 1988. p. 119.

ter. Others bind their anxiety by trying to arrange, control, and dominate the lives of others, be they their mate, their children, their co-workers, or even their friends. This is one reason why intimate relationships, inside or outside of legal marriage, can be so difficult and so challenging. Others bind by becoming obsessed with daily routines. Still others bind their anxiety by the fanatical pursuit of spectator sports or a by fanatical pursuit of participatory sports.

I recall offering therapy to a highly competitive football fan who appeared to be in a state of depression after a difficult loss. It was about the second or third session in the treatment and most of the focus had been on problems he was having, both in his family and at his place of work. On this occasion he was discussing the game and moaning about how depressed he was over the defeat. After listening to a rather long criticism of the coach, I finally asked him: "Steve, if your team had won today, what would you be depressed about *right this very minute?*" (I was fairly certain his first answer would be "nothing.") Steve fought me on this but I insisted he chew on the question until our next session. In the next session, and for the first time, he dealt with his depression. It seemed that depression only hit him after something happened to "unbind" his anxiety. We worked on how Steve would seem to become more anxious and depressed after his favorite teams lost. He slowly began to see how winning helped him keep his anxiety at a safe and comfortable distance. (Of course, after this insight, it became our challenge, his and mine, to explore other ways to deal with his depression and anxiety.)

Have you ever wondered about people who absolutely appear to be wedded to their work? Have we any idea how many people could not function if they did not have their work? They work even though they are well off. They work because they enjoy it. They work because of the daily challenge. But some work because they are afraid to stop working! Some work to escape something. Some work to fill their otherwise empty hours. If I were to suggest to them that their work served to bind their anxiety, they would no doubt scoff at me and perhaps question my parentage!. Nevertheless, I could well be right-on!

The truth is that we bind anxiety via our leisure time pursuits, our interests, our hobbies, our pet projects. We bind our anxiety through eating, drugging, drinking, flirting, and sexing. We bind our anxiety by establishing friendships and by creating short-term as well as lasting relationships.

The reader may well be asking, "So what is wrong with all that, as long as one is moral and respectful of others?" There is nothing wrong with all that. As you say, as long as one is moral and respectful of others? Binding anxiety is not wrong. It is really a-moral. That is, it is neither right nor wrong! It simply is! It is right to the extent that we must bind a certain amount of anxiety or we could not function as responsible persons. It is wrong if we bind ourselves up so tight that we cannot function or remain in quality relationships.

Now, we are at the key point of this excursus on binding. One of the most powerful ways we bind our anxiety is via our beliefs and our belief systems. We will devote all of Chapter 7 to the importance of our belief system but for now we need to focus on how beliefs serve to bind our anxiety. Usually well hidden from ourselves, we choose (or are we driven) to believe certain things not just for what the belief holds to be true, but rather for what the holding of this belief does for us. If I believe that I have been treated very badly in this life, it is very logical that my internal feelings of anger, hostility and even hatred be siphoned off into some sort of a neutral zone where I may safely imagine terrible things happening to those who have made my life miserable. Perhaps I will develop a vivid sense of an afterlife where the unjust of this world will receive their due. Perhaps my keen sense of personal injustice and maltreatment will lead me to believe in a personal hell where my tormentors will be punished and tortured. Perhaps

I simply choose to believe that somewhere the books of life will balance out.

If, on the other hand, I am a strong believer, who, with Micah of old, believes in "doing justice, loving kindness, and walking humbly with thy god" (Micah 6:8), then, my belief may well direct me into a type of social mission, perhaps the Peace Corps, or perhaps a vocation with religious overtones (or perhaps not), but the end result ought to be that I gain an inner peace and a sense of meaningful involvement. My anxiety will have been "bound" in a perfectly reasonable and responsible way.

Our beliefs are powerful binders be they religious beliefs, political beliefs, or beliefs about proper social décor and social etiquette. Certainly, we all know fanatical patriots on the right side of the political spectrum who insinuate that those on the left are godless communists who should leave this country rather than criticize it. We may also know radicals on the left who show no love or respect for those on the right. Indeed, we have seen the same kind of political venom in local school board elections over the issues of abortion, sex education, and advocates of evolution versus so-called believers in "intelligent design."

In fact, our disparate and opposing beliefs probably serve to bind us into bands, groups, nationalities, religions, and all sorts of cultural and sub-cultural divisions. And the pay-off is almost universally similar, i.e., we gain strong emotional security and strength of conviction via our emotional bonding with like believers and fellow compatriots, regardless of the issue at hand.

You are now probably fully aware as to where we are headed with this idea of one's beliefs as binders of anxiety. Death is the primal fear. In the facing of life, we can never escape the fact that we will one day die.[35] It is this knowledge which is the source of much of our anxiety. It is not simply and only a death anxiety but an anxiety attached to existence itself. It is the *angst der kreatur* as well as the failure to accept a certain amount of anxiety as being normal, i.e., as being a necessary correlate of the freedom of choice and the challenges of life on this planet.

This is the main theme of Erich Fromm's *Escape From Freedom* in which he shows clearly that many people will do almost anything in order to escape from the insecurity and anxiety of freedom. They will bow to an authoritarian person, or to an authoritarian church, or to the regime of any supposed superior who, in exchange for obedience and servitude, will bestow security and safety. As Fromm states in Foreword II, "...as the analysis in *Escape From Freedom* attempts to show, modern man still is anxious and tempted to surrender his freedom to dictators of all kinds, or to lose it by transforming himself into a small cog in the machine, well fed, and well clothed, yet not a free man but an automaton."[36]

If the reader will recall my tale from Chapter 1, what happened to me was that in losing my faith in god, I lost the prime object to which my anxiety had been securely bound. When this happened it was like cutting my life line or my tether to my security figureheads (or security blankets), god and Jesus. When my tether was cut — when my self-hood security system was abolished — my anxiety broke out all over the place. The key thought, here, is loss. When the protective and binding belief is lost (or destroyed, or fizzles out, or melts away, or is simply outgrown), then the entire self may be severely threatened.

---

35 Fear of death is one thing. Anxiety connected to the act of dying is quite another. It is one thing to say, "I do not fear death!" It is quite another thing to say, "I have no anxiety about extended death-bed illness, loss of functions and mental acuity."

36 Fromm, op. cit. *Escape From Freedom*, Foreword II. 1965. Also, Erich Fromm,1947. *Man For Himself*. New York: Holt, Rinehart & Winston.(*Man For Himself* is basically a continuation of *Escape From Freedom*.)

When we first come to the realization that there is no god and hence no basis for a faith that transcends nature, we may feel threatened to the core, as I was for a time. Of course, there may be increased anxiety about existence. Rest assured, this will run its course, especially as we learn to trust strongly in our own powers of thought and will. As we reconstruct our life we will learn a new way of being, a way that allows us to accept life on its own terms without artificial belief systems in the supernatural, without divine revelations, and without mythological authorities and shaman-like gurus.

Chapter 4. Loss

Ever since the events surrounding my leaving the ministry, I have believed that a great deal of what we call mental or emotional health has to do with how we handle or cope with loss. I see loss as underlying almost every theory of human development and every psychotherapeutic endeavor. Early childhood development is a transition from one stage to another with each stage or plateau involving losses and gains. Theories of aging often focus on the changes that come with ensuing years and the cumulative effect of mounting changes and losses. To be sure, a lot of the loss literature is just beneath the surface of stress literature, i.e., stress being the word of choice by many researchers and psychotherapists. To be technical about it, a vast number of stressor events are born of loss. Stress is not always loss but loss is almost always stressful.

Grief and the handling of grief are also closely associated with loss. In dealing with loss many researchers, psychotherapists, marriage/family therapists, and social workers will focus on grief work, recovery, and healing. Since the central theme of this book is learning to cope with the loss of god and loss of faith we will continue to keep these losses as our primary focus, with all other losses associated with human existence as a secondary focus. However, we need first to explore the subject of loss in general.

To this end I ask that you, the reader, join with me in listing instances of loss. We can categorize and classify them later. This list will be just an introductory beginning. The more you ponder the losses of life, the longer the list becomes. There is loss of innocence, youth, virginity, and dignity. There is the loss of money, status, role, popularity, prestige, and fame. There is the loss of mate, be it via divorce, infidelity, death, or irreconcilable differences — even if a couple remain married. There is the loss of children as they grow out of childhood into adolescence. There is the loss of closeness to parents as adolescents abandon their childhood ties and take on the rebellious attitudes of their peers and their sub-culture. Then there are the cumulative losses of our physical development such as the loss of teeth and tonsils. There is the possibility of the loss of appendages. There is the loss of bodily functions and the losses associated with aging such as loss of body tone, physical strength and energy, mental acuity, figure, and body silhouette. Not to mention loss of hearing, eyesight, hair and youthful physical attraction and sex appeal. There is loss of reproductive function including menopause, oophorectomy (removal of ovaries), hysterectomy, erectile dysfunction, ejaculatory incompetence, and losses due to miscarriage, stillbirth, and abortion. There is the loss of job, employment, or losing one's business. Let us not forget the loss of close friendship and the loss of support systems. There is the loss of hope, opportunity, ideals, and dreams. There is the loss of dogs, cats, and other pets. Finally, and most importantly for our purposes, there is the inevitable loss of life, the loss of parents, the loss of children (via disease, accidental death, and war), the loss of grandparents, relatives and other loved ones. And especially for those most interested in the central theme of these pages, there is the loss of god, the loss of faith, and perhaps loss of the religious institutions supporting belief in God, Yahweh, or Allah, i.e., loss of the church, the synagogue, and the mosque.

Normative Versus Catastrophic

Please allow me to be academic for several paragraphs and first divide loss into normative loss and catastrophic loss.[37] When we think of normative loss, what comes to our mind? If you look back to the previous paragraph, you will immediately be able to label some of the losses as normative and some as catastrophic. While it is a matter of operational definition, catastrophic loss is usually characterized as being "sudden, unpredictable, and overwhelming," while normal losses are more likely to arise out of developmental and physiological growth and cumulative setbacks and deterioration. Death, regardless of whether it is accidental and sudden or a slow evolution, is almost always considered to be a catastrophic loss.[38]

If we allow our imaginations to run free, we may quickly focus on natural disasters as distinguished from man-made disasters. Loss due to earthquakes, fires, floods, famines, droughts, dust storms, tornadoes, and hurricanes are all of a kind whereas loss due to warfare, machine or mechanical malfunction such as automobile breakdown or aircraft flameout and ship capsizing is of a different kind. There are also losses due to mine explosions and cave-ins, losses due to poorly designed products of all descriptions. There are many losses that stem from the interaction of both natural phenomena and human error, unintentional mistakes and miscalculation, such as when a bridge collapses due to rising flood wa-

---

37 Charles R. Figley and Hamilton I. McCubbin. *Stress and the Family*, Volume I, *Coping With Normative Transitions*, and Volume II, *Coping With Catastrophe*. New York: Brunner/Mazel, Publishers. 1983. In this series death is considered to be a catastrophic loss.
38 Ibid. p. V, Preface to the Series.

ters, which in turn are due to back flooding because of the blacktop jungles causing accelerated run-off in our cities and communities. There are also poorly designed and poorly located — or poorly maintained — dams. Additionally, there are losses that result from the unpredictable patterns of natural species such as the migration of birds.[39]

While there is little question about the potential devastation associated with natural catastrophe, we may fail to see that human activity intended to be in harmony with nature often turns out to be disharmonious. To what extent has strip mining without reclamation of the land contributed to catastrophic flooding? As we move toward increasing use of wind power, do we understand possible effects of giant wind machines on wildlife? How about damming and the effect on bodies of water and the rich feeding grounds they provide for fish and other creatures? Great environmental and ethical issues face the populations of all the nations of the earth. These include, among many others, the use of fossil fuels, the depletion of wood forest reserves, and drilling for oil and natural gas. Possibilities for future environmental protection usually involve both loss and gain of some kind and will likely have direct and indirect impacts on all creatures on the planet, including all of us.

---

39 January 15, 2009. U. S. Airways Flight 1529, an Airbus A320, just after take-off, encountered a flock of birds, some of which were ingested into the two jet engines causing complete shutdown and loss of power, the aircraft being expertly guided to touch down in the Hudson River, with immediate aid and rescue by nearby watercraft. Here, nature and man are probably equally implicated in the creation of a near catastrophic disaster, although the captain and crew of the aircraft and the rescue by the watercraft personnel proved, in this case, to have made the key difference in saving 155 lives plus the possible thousands who would possibly have perished had the plane crashed into adjacent high-rises and apartment complexes. Also, it should be noted, the weather was clear and the water calm. October 28-30, 2012. Hurricane *Sandy* devastates the eastern seaboard, especially the New Jersey coast, and wreaks havoc with the greater New York City area.

Replaceable Versus Irreplaceable

Another factor that we must consider as we look at the broad subject of loss is whether or not the loss is replaceable or irreplaceable. Arms and legs do not grow back. Literally speaking, people do not come back from the grave. (Although, as we know, the memory of loved ones and feared ones can easily come back to disturb the living.) While people do not come back from the grave, a widow or widower can sometimes remarry, thus, in a sense, replacing the previous mate in the role of husband or wife. People do replace (to some extent) deceased children by conceiving and giving birth to a new child.[40] In discussing the extent to which a person is replaceable, we need to be clear whether we are talking about the finality of a particular death, which is always irreplaceable, or the possibility of finding a new person to fill the role or status within the family that was left void. The bottom line is that a role can be filled by someone else, but there is no substitute for the individual person; the deceased person himself or herself cannot be replaced.

Many lesser losses are replaceable, again at least to some extent. If a living, human body part cannot be replaced in every detail, it often can be replaced with a satisfactory substitute. Increasingly some body parts are replaceable such as knees, hip joints, cataract lenses, even legs, feet, and arms. Allegedly George Washington had artificial teeth fashioned from wood. Today, we have dental plates, partials, bridges, and implants. Modern plastic surgery does wondrous things for the human body. Perhaps with greater knowledge about DNA and stem cell research, it will be possible someday even to grow replacements for some body parts.

Some losses may be directly replaceable, such as a car that has been totaled, or any other kind of man-made product of

---

40 The writer is the son of a replacement child. My father was conceived only after the death of his older sister. Had the infant sister not died, so my family legend maintains, my dad would not have been conceived.

mass production. If a manufactured article is no longer in production, it has usually been replaced by a more modern and up to date version; and as long as we can afford to buy the new one, we may benefit from the change. Other losses are irreplaceable, such as when a fire destroys one's belongings including treasured photographs, letters, diaries, mementos and heirlooms.

When we lose our job or our means of earning a living, we often cannot find a direct replacement due to the changing environment and needs of the workplace. Many jobs no longer exist. Products that once required the expertise of a worker in a repair shop are now frequently discarded under the policy of planned obsolescence. Slowly our society has witnessed the disappearance of such repair shops, which means a loss of jobs and small businesses. And while the automobile has not replaced the bicycle, email has certainly reduced the volume of first-class mail.

More specifically to our task in coping with the loss of god, or as some would say, the loss of faith, we need to realize that we are dealing with a catastrophic loss that is not normative. It is both catastrophic and irreplaceable. Some would argue this point! They say that the idea of god is replaceable because humans have always been creative in replacing their broken idols and icons. John Calvin certainly believed that the human mind was a forge (some translate *factory*) for the creation of idols.[41] I would hold that, if the transcendent, monotheistic, omnipotent, omniscient, omnipresent force that millions of people refer to as "God" is no longer a viable force or object of faith, then, by definition, this force is irreplaceable.

While it is true that many do choose to deal with the loss of god by constructing some sort of substitute god force, it remains accurate to say that the god they are replacing is dead. We will look more carefully at this phenomenon in Chapter

---

41 John Calvin, *Institutes*. 1-11-8, "Hence, we may infer, that the human mind is, so to speak, a perpetual forge of idols."

8. Nevertheless, for most of us to construct a new god force is simply to create for ourselves an alternative object of worship. We find ourselves to be in the same old mold of trying to replace the irreplaceable. Instead of coping directly with the loss of god we fashion a new idol to worship. The King is dead. Long live the King. The Queen is dead. Long live the Queen. God is dead. Long live God.[42]

Death as Evolving or Sudden

Lurking in the back of most people's mind is the dread of what must come, more inescapable even than the tax man. The prospect of our own death, and the death of others whom we love and rely upon, can haunt us.

We mentioned earlier that death is almost always considered to be catastrophic. The reason for this is that while the natural demise of elders may seem to be a normative transition, in terms of the emptiness, the void their death brings, it remains catastrophic. That is why psychologists, philosophers, and anthropologists claim that death, for the decedent, is the most catastrophic event any of us face in this life. While we don't recall our birth, we have our entire lifetime, be it short or very long, to anticipate and contemplate the inevitable reality and finality of our death. Most of us tend to underestimate it. We like to think that reason and logic can trump emotional turmoil. This is why the repression of death is necessary, as Becker's book, *The Denial of Death*, points out. Simply put, humankind represses that which it most fears. "Consciousness of death is the primary repression."[43] "The final terror of self-consciousness is the knowledge of one's own

---

42 Of course, there is a major difference between believing we had really experienced God as being alive and real — and losing that, versus never having had a firm belief in any god; although in the second case there may also be a profound sense of pain, aloneness, and missing something that was needed.

43 Becker, op. cit., p. 96.

death, which is the peculiar sentence of man alone in the animal kingdom."[44]

The reader may now like to interject, "O.K., but the expected type of death, as when a person dies slowly of cancer or perhaps congestive heart failure, having lived a long life, can be less traumatic than sudden, unexpected and premature death." Indeed, perhaps we need to make a distinction between expected death and sudden, unexpected death. Clearly there is a difference between hearing of the death of a son or daughter, mother or father, in an automobile accident, air crash, or train crash, compared to hearing that death has come to an aged person who had been suffering unbearably with a severe and terminal malady over many weeks, months, or years. In the latter case, death had been expected. In this comparison between unexpected and expected death, both of which are catastrophic, we also touch on the outer limits of the insanity of warfare and other forms of intentional killing, be it called homicide, murder or suicide. Here, the horror is all the greater, because the massacre and slaughter involved are due to human planning and design, even if they are termed "collateral" damage.

For me, there are plenty of circumstances that might surround death that are far more difficult to deal with than expected death due to illness. To me, sudden and unexpected death is the most difficult to cope with in terms of grief work and ongoing acceptance. Having said this does not diminish the scope, the depth, and the breadth of the grief work necessary in the facing of expected death. But there is simply no way a therapist or minister, priest, ayatollah, or rabbi can, in good conscience, fail to be moved by the challenge of attempting to comfort a family that has just lost a member due to an accident, a natural disaster, or through crime or even a military or terrorist attack.

---

44 Becker, op. cit., p. 70.

Two Approaches in Dealing with Catastrophic and Irreplaceable Loss

The rational approach, sometimes called the Spock syndrome, from the character in the television show *Star Trek*, is an "ultra-reasonable" approach to dealing with catastrophic loss.[45] It is ultra reasonable because it applies all the principles of logic and reason to the reality of loss and then proceeds from there.[46] This approach is not wrong in itself, but if it is the only approach, it falls far short of the reality of loss caused by death, even expected and evolving death. Haven't you ever wondered why people seem to get stuck on either one or the other of the two poles of grief resolution? The rational pole is to be entirely in one's mind about the loss. The polar opposite, the emotional pole, is to remain entirely in one's viscera about the loss.

Evan is in his mid-fifties and he is having a difficult time accepting the death of his father. He knows very well that if his Dad had lingered longer, there would be a nursing home, total immobility, no quality of life or hope for recovery. All these factors tended to assuage Evan's grief for an hour or two but then he would retreat into a depression.

"I process this stuff in my head but I can't seem to get out of my funk. I know Dad is better off and I know he certainly — given the circumstances — would not wish to continue living. But why then...? It's just that..... Why can't I get off of this and get back to some degree of normalcy? After all, it's not as though I wasn't prepared for his death. I knew it was coming. And he really went quite peacefully and without much pain."

---

45 Virginia Satir. *The New Peoplemaking.* Mountain View California: Science and Behavior Books. 1988.(Chapter Seven)

46 McCubbin and Figley, op. cit, *Stress and the Family: Coping With Catastrophe.* Chapter 5, Death: "Family Adjustment to Loss", John F. Crosby and Nancy L Jose. Pp. 76-89.

The answer to Evan's question is not easy. It strikes at the very nature of loss due to bereavement. Evan's thought system may be functioning in full gear as he uses reasonable logic and hard facts to assure himself that life for his father had run its course. His father's body had simply given out. At the same time, Evan is absolutely unaware of the depth of his own grief. And that is the point. Evan thought he was prepared for the inevitable but in truth he was totally unprepared for the huge empty void that he experienced within himself in the weeks and months after his father's death. Evan thought that the grief could be explained away by using rational facts. But rational facts and the use of impeccable logic fail to address the big void down in the pit of Evan's abdomen. No matter how Evan explains the fact of his father's illness and death, he still experiences this abyss of nothingness. The tugging and the pain of emptiness deep down in the gut is the way our body expresses itself and experiences itself when we truly grieve for someone who had been very important and valuable to us.

After I attempted to get Evan to talk with his viscera, he protested that he and his dad had endured a fair amount of conflict over the years. "But you don't understand! While I miss him, it isn't as though we were all that close and buddy-buddy while he was alive. At times I was so mad at him I could've run him through!" Here again, Evan is using reason and logic to convince himself that the relationship was not all that great and therefore he should not be feeling this pain. This kind of thinking is far off the mark. The degree of anger we may feel toward the deceased is a sign of involvement with that person, right, wrong, or otherwise. Oftentimes the greater the amount of unresolved conflict with the decedent, the greater the challenge of grief resolution. In this sense the loss due to death is never the end of the story for the loved one experiencing the loss.

Evan is a man of superior logic and reason. Yet he had become very unreasonable and illogical when it came to seeing that his Dad's death, no matter how it is explained and understood and justified, has still left a sizable hole in Evan's life. His father, who was present and available, even if not always in tune with his son, is now gone! Dead! Forever! Extinct! The hole is there. The void is empty. No more words. No more fights. No more drinking beer together. What once was, is no more.

The reader may now be expecting me to say that all of a sudden Evan broke down and sobbed and cried, letting out tons of pent-up emotion, as if this were a movie or television drama. This did not happen. What did happen was that eventually I received a note — months after therapy had ended.

"Thanks. I don't know how or why but slowly I'm feeling better. I guess I failed to realize that understanding Dad's death was no substitute for deep down gut-wrenching missing him."

This note tells it all. It is profound. I think what happened was that Evan, in telling his tale to me, slowly stopped his head trip about understanding his Dad's demise. At the same time the reality of inner emptiness and loneliness came home to him in a new way. Evan began to feel the stark, naked, pain and emptiness, the hole in his abdomen. He finally allowed himself to feel the pain of loneliness due to the absence of someone whom he had always taken for granted. To escape such feelings, Evan had simply focused on the rational, i.e., on what most of us would readily accept as a logical, natural, and understandable death for ourselves. But it is also rational to understand that any great and meaningful loss will leave an emptiness that must be faced with courage, empathy, and understanding. If we wish to be truly "rational," we must come to terms with our emotional "limbic" system which demands to have its day.

I bring this chapter to a close by re-stating that fear of death is the primal fear and that the supreme ongoing anxiety is the anxiety of existence itself, replete with the ever-present possibility of loss in all its forms. This primal fear comes clos-est to us as we experience the loss of persons who are mean-ingful and valuable to us, regardless of whether their death is the expected final playing out of a life or a lightning-like ending that is totally unexpected — an evolved finality or a disastrous and horrendous tragedy. If the fear of death is the primal fear, then it follows that the primal loss is the loss of the self. We will return to this theme in later chapters.

In the aftermath of the loss of god, a catastrophic loss for those who have spent part of their life in worship and com-mitment to such a god, life is never to be dismissed in a light vein. As we shall see, life becomes more precious and mean-ingful than ever before. The awareness of the loss may be sud-den or slow in evolving, but the power of its impact on how we now make sense of our life and how we give meaning to our own existence is immeasurable. As I have said, the loss of this god is absolutely irreplaceable. In the facing of this loss we turn to the subject of courage.

CHAPTER 5. COURAGE

Courage sounds like a straightforward word indicating a basic human characteristic. A dictionary definition runs thus: "Mental or moral strength to venture, persevere, and withstand danger, fear, or difficulty." [47] For our purposes I prefer to define courage as the perseverance of will in the presence of mental and physical adversity, including the anxiety of suffering, meaninglessness, and the finality of non-existence. This courage does not come easily and that is the rub. Tillich says that "Courage is self-affirmation 'in-spite-of,' that is in spite of that which tends to prevent the self from affirming itself."[48] In order to understand Tillich's definition of courage, we need to delve into the entire overlay of Tillich's analysis of courage, non-being, and the anxiety of existence.

Paul Tillich and "The Courage To Be"

Tillich's *Courage To Be* stands as a classic contribution to the interdisciplinary literature embracing the worlds of the-

---

47 Merriam Webster's Collegiate Dictionary, Eleventh Edition.
48 Paul Tillich. *The Courage To Be*. New Haven: Yale University Press, 1952. p. 32..

ology and depth psychology.[49] My basic question is whether or not, and to what extent, Tillich's treatment of courage can be of any help in the aftermath of the loss of god.

Tillich's analysis of courage depends first and foremost upon his analysis of anxiety. He sees three basic kinds of anxiety:

1. The anxiety of fate and death (Ontic anxiety)

2. The anxiety of emptiness and meaninglessness (Spiritual anxiety)

3. The anxiety of guilt and condemnation (Moral anxiety)[50]

For our purpose we need to be aware that all three types of anxiety are with each of us in blending proportions every day of our lives.

The first anxiety, the ontic or "being," is the anxiety of fate and death. "Fate and death are the way in which our ontic self-affirmation is threatened by nonbeing. 'Ontic,' from the Greek *on*, 'being,' means the basic self-affirmation of a being in its simple existence. (Onto-logical designates the philosophical analysis of the nature of being.) The anxiety of fate and death is most basic, most universal, and inescapable. All attempts to argue it away are futile...everybody is aware of the complete loss of self which physiological extinction implies. The unsophisticated mind knows instinctively what sophisticated ontology formulates..."[51] "Nonbeing is omnipresent and produces anxiety even where an immediate threat of death is absent."[52]

The second anxiety, the anxiety of emptiness and meaninglessness, "is anxiety about the loss of an ultimate concern, of a meaning which gives meaning to all meanings. This anxi-

---

49 A term arising after the advent of the Freudians, the Adlerians, and the Jungians, referring to the psychology, especially psychoanalysis, that attempts to understand the unconscious functions and forces of the human mind.

50 For our purposes I think it is best to bypass this historical part of Tillich's theme simply because Tillich's main premises do not depend on the accuracy of his historical analysis.

51 Tillich, op. cit., p. 42.

52 Ibid. p. 45.

ety is aroused by the loss of a spiritual center, of an answer, however symbolic and indirect, to the question of the meaning of existence."[53] For our purposes, when Tillich refers to a meaning which gives meaning to all meanings, he is referring to the question of the reality of a god or supreme force. Indeed, this strikes at the core of our present endeavor in this book because the loss about which I spoke in Chapter 1 is the loss of god and the consequent loss of meaning in life. Tillich goes on to say: "But a spiritual center cannot be produced intentionally, and the attempt to produce it only produces deeper anxiety. The anxiety of emptiness drives us to the abyss of meaninglessness."[54] In Chapter 8, we will address the philosophical-psychological movement known as *Constructivism*, wherein we learn to create reality. Here Tillich is saying quite bluntly that the harder we try to create a new god or a new version of god (a spiritual center) the deeper becomes our anxiety.

The third anxiety is the anxiety of guilt and condemnation. "Nonbeing threatens from a third side; it threatens man's moral self-affirmation. Man's being, ontic as well as spiritual, is not only given to him but also demanded of him. He is responsible for it: literally, he is required to answer, if he is asked, what he has made of himself. He who asks him is his judge, namely he himself, who at the same time stands against him. This situation produces the anxiety which, in relative terms, is the anxiety of guilt; in absolute terms, the anxiety of self-rejection or condemnation."[55] The guilt Tillich here refers to is the guilt we inflict upon ourselves for failing to fulfill our potential.

None of these types of anxiety can be separated from the others. They are each overlapping and in and out of each other. Yet they all three underlie the human dilemma of facing

---

53 Ibid. p. 47.
54 Ibid. p. 48.
55 Ibid. p. 51-52.

death, facing life, and facing ever-present anxiety. Along with these there is the threat of meaninglessness, failure, and guilt.

We must now ask: What does Tillich do with this analysis? First, he holds to the concept that "anxiety is the state in which a being is aware of its possible nonbeing. The same statement, in a shorter form, would read: anxiety is the existential awareness of nonbeing. 'Existential' in this sentence means that it is *not the abstract knowledge of nonbeing which produces anxiety but the awareness that nonbeing is a part of one's own being.* It is not the realization of universal transitoriness, not even the experience of the death of others, but the impression of these events on the *always latent awareness of our own having to die that produces anxiety*"[56] (italics added.) Tillich claims that humans cannot escape the basic anxiety. "The basic anxiety, the anxiety of a finite being about the threat of nonbeing, cannot be eliminated. It belongs to existence itself."[57]

Tillich's analysis of courage reflects the human condition in a powerful way. Tillich claims that, "Courage does not remove anxiety. Since anxiety is existential, it cannot be removed. But courage takes the anxiety of nonbeing into itself." Courage is self-affirmation 'in spite-of,' namely in spite of nonbeing. In self-affirmation he who acts courageously takes the anxiety of nonbeing upon himself."[58] In short, the courage to be is the courage to affirm oneself in the face of non-existence, nothingness, loss of meaning and purpose, and sometimes defeat.

In my personal attempt to learn and practice courage as heretofore described by Tillich, I found the most helpful and hopeful answers in the concepts of *self-affirmation* and *self-assertion* as outlined by Rollo May and in the search for meaning in human existence as elaborated by Viktor Frankl.

---

56 Ibid. p. 35.
57 Ibid. p.39.
58 Ibid. p. 66.

Rollo May and the Levels of Power

Rollo May outlines five levels of power with each successive level being cumulative. The second level builds on the first, the power to be. The third builds on the second, the power to affirm oneself. The fourth builds on the third, the power to assert oneself. The fifth builds on the fourth, the power to aggress. The final power is the power to violate. The fifth power is the ultimate destructive force common to individuals and societies, nationalities and cultures.[59]

The power to be is the initial level because it has to do with the matter of physical existence beginning at conception. The human infant begins as a zygote and evolves into an embryo. If everything progresses well the embryo becomes a fetus and at the end of the nine month gestation period it proceeds to pass into the birth canal and becomes a living human neonate. For May, the power to be is basic and elemental, a level of power every living human being has successfully negotiated, either via natural birth through the vaginal birth canal or by Cesarean Section, the surgical removal of the fetus. May says, "This power can be seen in the newborn infant — he can cry and violently wave his arms as signs of the discomfort within himself, demanding that his hunger or other needs be met. Whether we like it or not, power is central in the development in this infant of what we call personality... The power to be is neither good nor evil; it is prior to them. But it is *not* neutral. It must be lived out or neurosis, psychosis, or violence will result."[60]

---

59 May's analysis extends well beyond the individual. He focuses on the minorities of societies who have been enslaved, trodden upon, or otherwise deprived of life, liberty, and the pursuit of happiness. As the sub-title of his study of violence suggests, *Power and Innocence: A Search for the Sources of Violence* is an attempt to understand and develop the theme of power by attempting to trace how individuals learn and fail to learn self-power both in their individual lives and in their roles within society.

60 Rollo May. *Power and Innocence: A Search for the Sources of Violence.* New York: W. W. Norton & Company. 1972. p. 40.

The reader will recognize that May's second level of power, the power to affirm oneself, is the level that we wish to compare with Tillich's emphasis on self-affirmation. According to May, "Every being has the need not only to be but to affirm his own being. This is especially significant for the human organism, for it is gifted with, or condemned to, self-consciousness. This consciousness is not inborn but begins to develop in the infant after a few weeks. It is not fully developed for several years, and, indeed, continues developing throughout life. [61]

Self-affirmation is something that needs to be taught and encouraged with exemplars and role models, parents and teachers. We all need to be disabused of the silly and outrageous belief that it is wrong to love yourself. Self-love and self-esteem are the essential correlates of courage and self-affirmation. Was it poor parenting, poor theology, or poor elementary and higher public education that somehow failed to convey the truth of the message of self-respect and self-affirmation? Again, May states: "Inherent in power-to-be is the need to affirm one's own being. This, the second level in our spectrum, is the quiet, non-dramatic form of self-belief. It arises from an original feeling of worth imparted to the infant through the love of a parent or parents in the early months... It is self-affirmation that gives the staying capacity and depth to one's power to be."[62]

Mays's third level is self-assertion. He states: "When self-affirmation meets resistance we make greater effort, we give power to our stance, making clear what we are and what we believe; we state it now against opposition. This is *self-assertion*, the third phase. It is a stronger form of behavior than self-affirmation, and it is more overt. It is a potentiality in all of us that we react to attack. We make it unavoidable that the

---

61 Ibid. p. 40-41.
62 Ibid. p.137-138.

others see us as we cry: 'Here I am; I demand that you notice me!'"[63]

I often describe self-assertion as protecting my own life space. It is as if I were saying: "I am not aggressing into your life space, but I am not going to let you invade my life space. I mean no harm to you, but I am a force to be reckoned with if you insist on treading on me or walking over me." I think May is right on the mark when he claims, "Power becomes actualized in those situations in which opposition is overcome."[64]

The fourth level of power is aggression. "When self-assertion is blocked over a period of time...this stronger form of reaction tends to develop...In contrast to self-assertion, which is drawing a line at a certain point and insisting 'This is me; this is mine,' aggression is a moving into the positions of power or prestige or the territory of another and taking possession of some of it for one's self...this is a phase of behavior that in every person exists as a potentiality, and in the right situation it can be whipped into action."[65]

I characterize aggression as a move into the other person's life space. This move may be justified or not, but the individual has come to feel that such a move toward the other is warranted and necessary in order to protect the self. While I do not deny that there are times when courage may require a measure of aggression, I tend to hold strong the belief that greater amounts of self-affirmation and self-assertion could serve to reduce the need for aggression.

The final level of power is the use of violence. "Finally, when all efforts toward aggression are ineffective, there occurs the ultimate explosion known as *violence*. Violence is largely physical because the other phases, which can involve reasoning or persuasion, have been, *ipso facto* blocked off. In typical cases, the stimulus transmitted from the environment

63 Ibid. p.41.
64 Ibid. p.144.
65 Ibid. p.42.

to the individual is translated directly into the violent impulse to strike, with the cerebrum being bypassed."[66]

In short, when we perceive our position as hopeless, we are
much more likely to become violent. May states: "As we make
people powerless, we promote their violence rather than its
control. Deeds of violence in our society are performed largely
by those trying to establish their self-esteem, to defend their
self-image, and to demonstrate that they, too, are significant...
As Hannah Arendt has so well said, violence is the expression
of impotence."[67]

One need go no further than observe recess at the local
middle school to see the bully effect of both boys and girls as
they physically cross the line between aggression and the doing of violence. Admittedly, sometimes the line between aggression and violence is quite vague. It is probably accurate to
say that all violence includes aggression but not all aggression
need be violent.

I find in May's analysis of the five levels of power a fundamental clue to the nature of courage. In my view courage is
primarily the cumulative ability to affirm and assert oneself.
I repeat, violent people are usually the helpless people who
have failed to learn a healthy measure of self-affirmation, self-
assertion, and limited aggression. I do not wish to overem-
phasize the fourth level, the level of aggression. I only wish
to point out that on occasion it is a necessary ingredient of
courage.

As we have seen, Tillich talked about self-affirmation as
being the essential ingredient of courage. I agree with Tillich
in his analysis of courage and how we need to take the anxiety of fate and death, meaninglessness and emptiness, and
guilt and condemnation into ourselves. Further, following
Rollo May, I believe that our continued learning and practice

66 Ibid. p.43.
67 Ibid. p.23.

of self-affirmation and self-assertion is precisely the most logical and psychologically sound way of becoming courageous.

In the aftermath of my 'break' with god, I daily attempted to live courageously by redefining myself in terms of self-affirmation and self-assertion. In my personal struggle for survival after the loss of god I took every opportunity to affirm and assert my self-hood. Remember, I had previously allowed my identity to be merged and melded with the Christ figure, i.e., "For me to live is Christ and to die is gain" (Philippians 1:21). "It is no longer I who live, but Christ who lives in me" (Galatians 2:20).

Viktor Frankl and the Quest for Meaning

Tillich's negatives — death, meaninglessness, and guilt are collectively addressed by Viktor Frankl. Frankl was a World War II survivor of Auschwitz. His experience at Auschwitz re-affirmed the thesis of his first book, *The Doctor and the Soul*, the manuscript of which was taken from him at Auschwitz and had to be re-written from memory.[68] Frankl coined the term, *Logotherapy*, or *meaning therapy*, in contrast to psychotherapy and psychoanalysis, because Frankl's fundamental belief was that when an individual can define specific meanings and purposes for his existence he can endure. Freud is noted for his *Will to Pleasure*. Adler is noted for his *Will to Power*. Frankl is noted for his *Will to Meaning*.[69]

In short, Frankl sees men and women as meaning-makers. While humans may ascribe general meaning to their existence, including religious expressions of cosmic purpose, it is in the identification and definition of *particular* purpose and meaning in which humans find the strength of resolve and the

---

68 Viktor E. Frankl. *The Doctor and the Soul: From Psychotherapy to Logotherapy.* Alfred A. Knopf, Inc. 1946.

69 Viktor Frankl. *Man's Search For Meaning.* (Originally published as *From Death Camp to Existentialism*). Boston: Beacon Press. 1959. (Washington Square Press, Edition. 1963, 153.) New York: Simon & Schuster)

strength of courage to exist, especially in the face of despair, self doubt, and immeasurable amounts of both physical and mental and emotional suffering. One of the meanings of the Greek word, *logos*, is *meaning*. The purpose of *logotherapy* is to help the client by challenging her or him to detect, discover, invent, and create meaning and purpose for oneself. Frankl builds on Nietzsche: "There is much wisdom in the words of Nietzsche: He who has a *why* to live for can bear almost any *how*. I can see in these words a motto that holds true for any psychotherapy. In the Nazi concentration camps, one could have witnessed (and this was later confirmed by American psychiatrists both in Japan and Korea) that those who knew that there was a task waiting for them to fulfill were most apt to survive."[70]

Frankl describes the *existential vacuum*: "I shall now turn to the detrimental influence of that feeling of which so many patients complain today, namely the feeling of the total and ultimate meaninglessness of their lives. They lack the awareness of a meaning worth living for. They are haunted by the experience of their inner emptiness, a void within themselves: they are caught in that situation which I have called the 'existential vacuum.'"[71] Frankl continues: "Sometimes the frustrated will to meaning is vicariously compensated for by a will to power, including the most primitive form of the will to power, the will to money. In other cases, the place of frustrated will to meaning is taken by the will to pleasure. That is why existential frustration often eventuates in sexual compensation. We can observe, in such cases, that the sexual libido becomes rampant in the existential vacuum."[72]

Frankl comments that every age has its own "collective neurosis...The existential vacuum that is the mass neurosis of the present time, can be described as a private and personal

---

70 Ibid. p. 164-165.
71 Ibid. p. 167.
72 Ibid. p.170.

form of *nihilism;* for nihilism can be defined as the contention that being has no meaning."[73] In Frankl's will to meaning we see that Tillich's meaninglessness and emptiness is now addressed in a direct way. The courage to be is the courage to address the purpose and direction of one's own life. The courage to be is to see clearly how easily our western materialistic culture has seduced us into the pseudo security of money and wealth, pleasure, and immunity to pain and suffering via drugs, sex, and alcohol.

Logotherapy is not an easy therapy. The therapist sometimes becomes quite active by challenging the client with thoughts and ideas and suggestions the client might prefer not to hear. Logotherapy is direct, often brief in duration, and relatively free of dream analysis and attempts to discover the influences of the unconscious. In short, logotherapy is hands-on training for the learning of courage in the face of guilt, despair, meaninglessness, and emptiness. As such, it addresses the anxiety of non-being and becomes an ally in the learning of the courage to be.

In the aftermath of belief in god, we will begin to learn and practice a new kind of courage, a courage rooted in our own ability and willfulness to affirm and assert ourselves. This endeavor includes our quest for purpose and meaning in our own daily existence.

At this point in the reconstructing of our life without god, we shift gears and enter the realm of the self, for it is the self that constitutes who and what we are, and it is the self that incorporates the courage of self-affirmation, self-assertion, and self-definition.

---

73 Ibid. p.204.

Chapter 6. Self

The *self* is perhaps the most researched and theorized sub-topic in the arena of the psychology of human development. Literally, many thousands of journal articles, papers and books form a treasure trove of authoritative resources. And it goes back beyond early psychology to the ancients and their philosophical underpinnings. We should ask even before we begin: Are we talking about the *mind* of humans, the *soul* of humans, or the *spirit* of humans? Or are these inseparable? In short, what do we mean by the *self*?

For our purposes in dealing with the crucial issues related to reconstructing a life after god, I have settled on the one approach which I believe to be most helpful. This does not mean that other approaches are wrong or of less merit. But I have found the Bowen approach to the self to be personally helpful as well as professionally useful in my role as a marriage and family therapist with a strong systems orientation. For our purposes, let's designate the *self* as that basic core of identity which shapes you as a unique human being. It may include soul or spirit but it is best understood as the matrix of one's conscious and unconscious feelings, thoughts, attitudes, and beliefs. It contains the total of our emotions and our intellect.

Differentiation and Fusion

Murray Bowen was a psychiatrist who pioneered his own theory of family systems. Bowen is known and probably best remembered for his phrase "undifferentiated family ego mass."[74] By this he means the fusion or emotional stuck-togetherness of members of a family with each other. Bowen believes that human emotions are primary. This is to say that the emotional system precedes the intellectual system, and hence we are first and foremost creatures of our emotions.[75]

According to Bowen it takes strength, insight, and determination to live a life wherein the intellect reigns over the impulsiveness of the emotions, resisting the tendency to allow them to be fused together.

> Emotional functioning includes the automatic forces that govern protoplasmic life. It includes the force that biology defines as instinct, reproduction, the automatic activity controlled by the automatic nervous system, subjective emotional and feeling states, and the forces that govern relationship systems. ... There are varying degrees of 'fusion' between the emotional and intellectual systems in the human. The greater the fusion, the more the life is governed by automatic emotional forces that operate, despite man's intellectual verbalization to the contrary. The individual is fused into the emotional fusions of people around him. The greater the fusion, the more man is vulnerable to physical illness, emotional illness, and social illness, and the less he is able to consciously control his own life. In spite of the elemental power of the limbic system, it is possible for man to discriminate between the emotions and the intellect and to slowly gain more conscious control of emotional functioning.[76]

As we proceed to flesh out the difference between an undifferentiated human being and a differentiated one, we need

---

74 Murray Bowen, *Family Therapy In Clinical Practice*. New York: Jason Aronson. 1985. p. 363.
75 Ibid. p.305.
76 Ibid .p .305.

first to be reminded that families and couples and all other relationships, including work and professional relationships, may be filled with conflict, animosity, jealousy, envy, rivalry, competition, spite, and even hate. (Did I leave anything out?) The point is that people often fail to realize that these feelings can be the powerful glue that keeps everyone dynamically involved with each other and hence, stuck together. The undifferentiated family ego mass is not to be thought of as a "glued together, everybody loves each other, look how sweet we all are, look how much we take care of each other," type of situation. It may be that, but more likely the undifferentiated family ego mass is closer to a tinder box, ready to explode at the slightest provocation or the slightest attempt on someone's part to break away from the fusion and enmeshment.

A family's style and mode of handling conflict can be one of the most telling factors in determining the degree of differentiation its members have from each other. How a family fights together, even families that appear to be well-adjusted and free of conflict, as well as families of divorce, separation, division, and alienation, is an indicator of the level of differentiation. If the nature of the conflict rarely changes and the tone of the relationship is constantly negative and cutting, full of barbs, put-downs, and insults, then one can be fairly certain that the undifferentiated ego mass is well glued. Only a fairly well differentiated person will be able to break away from such fusion.

Differentiation is a key term with Bowen, referring to that process by which an individual is able to do two things: 1. To functionally separate the 'feeling' system from the 'thinking' system, and, 2. To function in an emotionally bonded way with one's fellow family members without compromising one's autonomous selfhood; in other words, breaking away, yet remaining part of, the fused reality. This means that you can disagree with others on many levels without becoming emotionally wrought-up or hooked into negativity. This involves the ability to be in relationship without being someone other than who you are and what you are, i.e., an authentic self.

Bowen describes differentiation: "The concept defines people according to the degree of fusion, or differentiation, between emotional and intellectual functioning. This characteristic is so universal it can be used as a way of categorizing all people on a single continuum. At the low extreme are those whose emotions and intellect are so fused that their lives are dominated by the automatic emotional system... At the other extreme are those who are more differentiated. It is impossible for there to be more than relative separation between emotional and intellectual functioning, but those whose intellectual functioning can retain relative autonomy in periods of stress are more flexible, more adaptable, and more independent of the emotionality about them."[77]

According to Bowen, the overriding challenge in growing out of childhood and adolescence is to separate oneself from the undifferentiated family ego mass.[78] "People tend to marry partners who have identical levels of differentiation of self. When the well differentiated person marries a spouse with an equally high level of identity, the spouses are able to maintain clear individuality and at the same time to have an intense, mature, nonthreatening emotional closeness."[79] Highly differentiated people are able to remain relatively autonomous as they share their lives, while people with relatively low levels of differentiation often have great difficulty in achieving and maintaining emotional independence because they remain glued into a mass of feeling and undifferentiated intellect.

For clinical and diagnostic purposes Bowen created a scale ranging from 0 to 100 with 0-25 being highly and intensely fused people, 25–50 moderate levels of differentiation with

---

77 Ibid. p.362.
78 Ibid. p.123.
79 Ibid. p.124

some initial differentiation between the emotional and intellectual systems, 50–75 increasingly moderate to good differentiation with both systems functioning as a cooperative team, and 75–100 more hypothetical than real. Michael Kerr states: "Rare people in the 85–95 range would have most of the characteristics" (ascribed to the very highly differentiated person).[80] Bowen remarks about the lower end of the scale: "At the fusion end of the spectrum, the intellect is so flooded by emotionality that the total life course is determined by the emotional process and by what 'feels right,' rather than by beliefs or opinions. The intellect exists as an appendage of the feeling system."[81]

The various gradients on the scale are not based on a pencil and paper instrument. There is no 'test' to take or forced-choice check list of personality traits. Rather, assignments on the Bowen scale are clinically subjective, being the result of extensive clinical interview profiles which Bowen claimed were remarkably accurate ten years later.[82] Bowen also believes that "the level of differentiation of a person is largely determined by the time he leaves the parental family and he attempts a life of his own."[83] Nevertheless, this is open to significant change if and when a person sees what kind of change is needed and then commits her or his energy to the task of differentiation by strengthening solid self.

Solid Self and Pseudo Self

The words *solid self* and *pseudo self* come from Murray Bowen, although it is likely these terms have been used in one way or another by both philosophers and psychologists for many years. In Bowen theory the concepts of *solid* and *pseudo* self

---

80 Michael Kerr and Murray Bowen. *Family Evaluation: An Approach Based on Bowen Theory.* New York: W. W. Norton & Company. 1988. p.106.

81 Bowen, op. cit., p.363.

82 Ibid. p.364.

83 Ibid. p.371

arise out of the concepts of fusion and differentiation, i.e., the relative strength and predominance of the emotional and intellectual systems. Bowen warns his readers: "Based on my experience with this concept, I believe that the level of solid self is lower, and of the pseudo-self is much higher in all of us than most are aware."[84]

"In periods of emotional intimacy, two pseudo-selfs will fuse into each other, one losing self to the other, who gains self. The solid self says, 'This is who I am, what I believe, what I stand for, and what I will do or will not do' in a given situation. The solid self is made up of clearly defined beliefs, opinions, convictions, and life principles. These are incorporated into self from one's own life experiences, by a process of intellectual reasoning and the careful consideration of the alternatives involved in the choice. In making the choice, one becomes responsible for self and the consequences."[85]

In contrast, the pseudo-self can be characterized in many different ways. Some would characterize it as underdog. Others as traitor mind, one-down, and as a non-productive self. It has been called a not-OK self, a weak self, an inferior self, a wimpy self. What Bowen and Kerr refer to as pseudo-self is similar to all of these. They all convey a self that is too ready to adapt to what others think it should be and do. The pseudo-self is eager to please and to placate. The pseudo-self will bind anxiety at every opportunity. Instead of dealing with issues and conflicts, it seeks to short-cut genuine peace by glossing over honest differences.

In Bowen's terms, pseudo-self is being enmeshed or fused within the family, or with one's mother or father. It is mired in the glue of the family or group and cannot think for itself or act on its own without the blessing or confirmation of authority. It lives by attachment and finds its security in being one-

---

84 Ibid. p. 366.
85 Ibid. p 364-365.

down and inferior, afraid to stand on its own or take the lead. The pseudo-self is a sham, a pretense, a cover, a chameleon.[86]

The pseudo-self is basically insecure and afraid. The pseudo-self seeks to avoid conflict and to protect itself by blending in with the social, political, or religious group. Because the pseudo-self is captive to the emotional sub-system, it will always retreat to the mass group-think that most fits her or his belief system. This mass group-think may be strongly political and may manifest social characteristics that are prejudicial and strongly biased toward inequality, severe punishment, and severe ostracism for those who stray from the group thought and behavioral norm. Many fundamentalist religious groups, Christian, Jewish, Muslim or other, celebrate the fusion of the group as it stands up to and attacks those who do not agree or are otherwise considered to be outsiders or representatives of the enemy camp. Far-right political enclaves also celebrate unchallenged authority and maintain a tight fusion amongst followers and believers. Amongst pseudo-selves, differentiation is considered to be anathema.

On a more personal level, excluding the extremes of fundamentalism and far right and far left politics, the pseudo-self will invariably sit on the fence until she or he determines which way the wind is blowing on controversial issues, or which way will be to his/her best security advantage. The pseudo-self will back off from aggression, even when it is called for. The pseudo-self will back down from asserting himself or herself, afraid to alienate or offend, even if it means compromising one's own values. In truth, the pseudo-self lacks courage to be, too often afraid even to affirm his or her own rights and thoughts and principles. Protection is sought in the group think and in the group involvement, be it the political party, the menagerie of clubs and fraternities, the church, mosque, or synagogue. Once again we see that in

---

86 Ibid. p. 365.

the lack of self-affirmation and self-assertion the pseudo-self shows an absence of courage.

In contrast to the pseudo-self, the solid self is not afraid to make mistakes. The solid self is not afraid to take a stand. Those with solid selves don't always have to be politically correct because they are strong enough to reassess their position in the light of different facts and emerging developments. The solid self can be quite at odds with others in regard to all kinds of beliefs and yet remain in good communication with opponents and adversaries. The solid self does not need to ridicule or attack or make fun of other people because the solid self sticks to the issues and employs the tools of critical thinking, reason, and measured circumspection to state his or her case. The solid self is far more likely to travel the road less taken, by thinking freely, creatively, and independently. Further, the solid self is far less likely than the pseudo self to hearken to the voice of authority or authority figures, whether political or religious.

Criticism and Self-Esteem

One of the most telling indications of pseudo-self is in how the individual responds to criticism, be it negative or positive criticism. Few of us like to be shown our flaws and errors, but such criticism is a necessary part of growing up and of becoming a better person. The over-sensitive pseudo-self is often simply crushed by any hint of negative criticism or evaluation.

Even the solid self probably doesn't relish the idea of criticism. But the solid self learns to accept input from others, even when it's not delivered with great tact, as part of growing maturity and self-improvement. Those athletes who have learned to accept coaching and criticism are often the ones who become the best players. Criticism, as I have said, may not be fun but it is a necessary part of learning to be a solid self. Talented musicians and artists, authors and playwrights, salesman and politicians have learned to be thick skinned as they absorb both negative and positive correction and criticism. This is solid self. Taking criticism is not easy, but if we are to develop solid self we must develop an attitude toward criticism that will work in our favor rather than against us. The respected Norman Vincent Peale is reputed to have said: "The trouble with most of us is that we would rather be ruined by praise than saved by criticism."

If we allow criticism to overwhelm us, and if we interpret it as a devastating and debilitating message that we are worthless or just plain incompetent, then we are bound to take refuge in pseudo-self. On the other hand, once we take on the challenge of creating solid self, we may soon discover that what others may say about us cannot finally hurt us unless we allow it. As a matter of fact, no one can have final power over me unless I somehow allow it, permit it, or tolerate it.

The entire subject of criticism is actually part of a greater argument that has to do with self-image and praise. The argument is centered upon the need for positive and strong self-image in children. On the one side are those who believe that parents should seize on the slightest opportunity to build up positive self image, no matter the truth or reality of the situation. The other side of the argument is that children see through false and non-authentic praise very quickly. Let us listen to David Walsh, writing in his book, *NO*, as he criticizes the self-esteem craze: "'Self-esteem is the key to happiness.' This mantra has emerged as an accepted truism of modern American culture. That's the reason you find raising children's *self-esteem* goals in the mission statement of school districts across the country. An entire industry has blossomed that guarantees 'enhanced self-esteem' to those who sign up for courses, subscribe to newsletters, or enroll in weekend retreats. That goal wouldn't be a problem if only we defined *self-*

esteem correctly. Most of what passes as self-esteem boosting, however, is *feel-good chatter* (italics added). The real deal is crucial to success and happiness, but real self-esteem is also more difficult to build and is directly tied to No."[87] Walsh hits the nail squarely when he discusses the absolute necessity for parental usage of the word, *No*. The very heart of self-discipline and the learning of authentic self-esteem is in parents and other teachers meting out discipline and the drawing of boundaries, not in softening down the challenges of accomplishment or the goals of creative pursuit.[88] What Walsh calls "feel-good chatter" is exactly that, i.e., an attempt to make a child, adolescent, or adult feel good even though he or she has failed miserably. We should save praise for those occasions when the person has accomplished or surmounted a genuine obstacle rather than making a simple or half-hearted effort to perform a task.

In the aftermath of god-belief, the individual is challenged to re-build and strengthen solid self. There is absolutely no short cut. The solid, differentiated self does not need the praise and fortifying "feel-good chatter" that often comes across as a pathetic attempt to help the injured child or adult feel good in defeat. The solid self needs only to believe in their own sense of judgment, in their own self-evaluation, in their own ability to think and evaluate various problems and situations. It does not mean one does not seek counsel and advice on occasion, but it does mean that each of us is an autonomous and self-reliant person who is able to separate our feelings from our best thought and then to act decisively and with conviction.

---

87 David Walsh. *No: Why Kids —of All Ages—Need to Hear It and Ways Parents Can Say It*. New York: Free Press 2007. p.57

88 I recommend David Walsh's book, *No*, as an absolute necessity in the armament of every parent and even grandparents. It has implications that go far beyond childhood and adolescence, even beyond young adulthood. Were I still teaching, I would insist on this book as essential reading in almost any functional course on human development and parenting.

Further, solid self prevents us from falling into subservience to an imagined god who will make us feel good about ourselves without actually having to learn the hard lessons of life and the necessary self-discipline that underlies the self-affirmation and courage of solid self.

Brief Summary of Steps to Solid Self

The following list is suggestive only. It is intended to stimulate thought as a precursor to action.

- Say "yes" to yourself and to life. You have as much right to be here as anyone else and you will not allow yourself to be minimized or defined by any other person, including husband, wife, son, daughter, friend, employer, mother, father, grandparent, or guardian.

- Once you have specified and itemized points of anger that recur in your thoughts, it is a good idea to quit feeding on them. If you have addressed these and you feel that you can do nothing more about them, then exercise self-discipline and stop going there. Solid self doesn't waste energy by carrying grudges and wallowing in the murky past.

- Believe and trust your own judgment. Inform yourself and attempt to learn all you can about any given matter or subject. At times you will seek help and advice on particular matters. Next, practice trusting your own "take" on things. If it turns out you were wrong or mistaken, simply acknowledge this to yourself and move on. Most of the time you will probably be right. Acknowledge this to yourself, also.

- Only pseudo self and weak-self people insist on always being right. People who insist on being right or who must always prove themselves right are simply showing how fragile their sense of self is. Only the solid, strong, and autonomous are able to admit when they are wrong. Only the solid, strong, and autonomous show an ongoing willingness to genuinely resubmit their own opinions to further scrutiny with the possibility that these opinions or conclusions could be wrong or misinformed. Only the solid, strong, and autonomous are willing to apologize and allow their humanity to show forth in empathy and sympathy.

- We are often told, "Don't take it personally!" Perhaps we feel slighted by someone. Or ignored. Or put down. My response: "Maybe it's not personal to you. To me, it is very personal." I encourage comments such as: "If we are to be friends, then we must respect each other by accepting our differences. If we are to be successful in this endeavor, then I insist on being treated as an equal. Otherwise, I'm out of here!"

- Solid self does not hesitate to draw boundaries when appropriate.

- Solid self does not allow others to intimidate me.

- In marriage: Sometimes solid self will protect itself by getting out! Sometimes solid self will insist on sticking it out, love not insisting on its own way.

- Reclaiming space and time-out: In love and marriage: "I love you. Right now I'm feeling hurt and rejected. I need my own space."

- In family: "I love you. You are my child. I forgive you. And... you are grounded for one week and no allowance for a month." Solid self does not confuse affection with approval, especially with children: "Yes, I love you. No, I do not approve of your behavior." Solid self does not confuse forgiveness with discipline and the need for a change of behavior.

Chapter 7. Belief

The Power of Belief

There is no doubt about it. What we humans believe determines how we live. Beliefs underlie just about everything that happens to us and that we cause to happen.

Beliefs have the power to change the world for ill or for better. Hitler had a strong belief about the Jews and Slavs and Gypsies, and homosexuals. John Adams, Benjamin Franklin, and Thomas Jefferson had a strong belief that democracy was possible. The Wright brothers, physicists, and space engineers all shared intense beliefs. So do the pioneers at NASA and the early astronauts who believed we could land humans on the moon and return them safely to earth. Einstein believed that the nucleus of the atom could be split and hence mastery of nuclear fission became a reality. At the same time, whole categories of Americans believe it is right to wage wars in faraway lands, incarcerate American citizens as well as foreigners indefinitely without trial

Many people use the words *faith* and *belief* interchangeably, although in strict definition they are different. I am reminded of the story of a young lad who was admiring a young man who was an accomplished tight rope walker. The rope went from either side of a very steep ravine. "So you believe I can cross this ravine on a tight rope?" the tight rope walker said to the admiring lad. "Oh yes! I've seen you do it," exclaimed the lad. "Well then," said the tightrope walker, "since you have seen me do it, would you like to climb up on my back and I'll piggy-back you across?" Of course, given this invitation, the lad was not at all sure about how strongly he believed in the tight-rope walker's ability. This is a rather simple story showing the difference between *belief about* and having *trust in*; it serves to illustrate the difference between trust as a simple statement of belief compared to trust as a total investing of one's faith in another person or another idea. Many beliefs that are a scourge on human society have become, in fact, articles of faith. I will leave it to linguistic researchers to formulate a distinction between belief and faith. What seems obvious, however, is that when a belief is accepted and adopted as one's own, it can quickly become a constructed reality which then may become an article of faith demanding total obedience and obeisance.

It is this transition between simple belief and a full investment of personal trust that causes so much pain and tragedy in the world. Beliefs become deeply personal and invested with meaning and purpose. Before you know what happened, people are killing other people.

New Beginnings

It is not enough to simply walk away from what you previously believed. The philosopher John Locke talked about the experiences of early life as having been written on a blank slate, the *tabula rasa*.[89] What we each must do, indeed, what we have been doing in these pages, is to question the early and not-so-early writings on this blank slate.

Let us begin by listing and questioning your basic beliefs. These beliefs are yours, so my questions are merely suggestive: You are the only qualified person to do this exercise. No one dare do it for you. You are now writing your own story. Here is an inventory of questions to get you started.

- What do you believe concerning the origin of the universe?

- Do you accept the so-called "Big Bang" hypothesis? Or "String Theory" hypothesis?

- Where do you stand on the question of a so-called "uncaused first cause"?

- What stands behind the uncaused first cause?

- If you no longer profess a belief in god, have you been tempted to create a god substitute?

- How do you reconcile the idea of a god substitute with the belief that ultimate reality can never be known, that no human being has ever returned from death, and that no philosopher or theologian has ever been able to establish god-belief on an empirical foundation?

- Do you accept the basic tenets of evolution, especially the concept of natural selection?

- What is your view of *Homo sapiens*? Are humans equal in their *Homo sapiens* commonality? Does this equality of personhood imply all *Homo sapiens* are equal in endowment of ability and brain power?

---

89 John Locke. *An Essay Concerning Human Understanding.* 1689. Book II, Chapter One, Section 2. Locke further writes: "It is easy to imagine how, by these means, it comes to pass that men worship the idols that have been set up in their minds; grow fond of the notions they have been long acquainted with there; and stamp the characters of divinity upon absurdities and errors; become zealous votaries to bulls and monkeys, and contend too, fight, and die in defense of their opinions." Book I, Chapter Two, Section 26.

- What could be the possible causes of violence among and between *Homo sapiens*? Is it self-protection or self aggrandizement, or other factors?

- What seems to cause some *Homo sapiens* to dominate and control others?

- Why is it that males historically have tended to dominate females in the great majority of known societies upon earth?

- In what ways do you think power and money (or wealth) are related in the human quest for security and the security of power?

- What is your view of the beginning of human life? Does the fertilization of an ovum by a sperm (a zygote) constitute human life? Or is a zygote, a fetus, or an embryo simply *potential* human life?

- What do you believe about stem cell research and the ethical question of using stem cells from non-viable embryos?

- What do you believe about population control, the use of birth control techniques and contraceptive devices, including oral contraceptives?

- What do you believe about marriage, divorce, cohabitation, civil law unions vs. civil law marriage?

- What do you believe about homosexuality?

- Do you believe same sex unions threaten marriage and family life?

- What do you believe about same sex couples having or adopting children?

- What do you believe regarding sexual ethics for consenting adults?

- What do you believe regarding sexual ethics for teenagers?

- What are your beliefs about welfare support for mothers who have no partner?

- What is your belief concerning the use of fossil fuels?

- Do you believe our planet is threatened by global warming?

- In what ways do you believe human beings can change in their interaction with the environment?

- What do you believe about alternative sources of energy such as water power, wind power, solar power?

A Question

In all candor and honesty, how many of your beliefs regarding items in the list above have substantially or significantly changed since god dropped off your radar? Of course, the god beliefs have changed and the idea of the uncaused first cause has probably changed as well. Other than these, which of your beliefs have changed?

I ask this question because it seems to me that gazillions of people think that without some belief or faith in god there will be no morality. These theists seem to believe that without god, there will be no human values or common morality and decency. On this issue, see the writings of Sam Harris, Richard Dawkins, Christopher Hitchens, Daniel Dennett, Dan Barker, and my own earlier work.[90] A thorough reading of these authors will go a long way toward putting to death the myth that god belief is a necessary pre-condition of ethics and morality. Likewise, a careful reading of the Old and New Testaments will make plain the morally bankrupt scriptural foundation for what is referred to as Judeo-Christian god-centered morality and family-centered values. We shall delve further into this question in Chapter 9.

---

90 Sam Harris. *The End of Faith: Religion, Terror, and the Future of Reason.* New York: W.W. Norton. 2004. Richard Dawkins. The God Delusion. Houghton Mifflin. 2006. Christopher Hitchens. *god is not Great: How Religion Poisons Everything.* New York: Twelve Publishing. 2007. Daniel Dennett. *Breaking The Spell: Religion As a Natural Phenomenon.* New York: Viking. 2006. Dan Barker. *godless: How an Evangelical Preacher Became One of America's Leading Atheists.* Berkeley, CA: Ulysses Press. 2008. John F. Crosby. *The Flipside of Godspeak: Theism As Constructed Reality.* Eugene, Oregon: Wipf and Stock.2007. (Chapters 6 and 7)

Beliefs and Constructs

Beliefs go a long way toward defining who you are. In Chapter 8 we will consider *constructivism* in greater detail. For now let me say that a belief tends to become a construct when you invest in it to the point of personal participation in the meaning of the belief. A construct is your perception of reality based upon a belief that is important to you. The construct fleshes out a series of related ideas based upon a belief. It shapes and forges these ideas into a network of related and congruent concepts. As an example of the difference between a belief and a construct I will return to my own experience of god.

In my former life, i.e., my 'Christian minister life,' I believed in god. But what did this belief mean? What did it imply? What did it entail? What did it require of me? What did it mean in terms of my family, my wife, my children? How did this belief color the landscape of daily life? How did it determine our family style of life, our manner of life, and our values? The god I believed in became, over time and with much cultivation, my constructed god which led to an entire set of propositions, of commitments, of demands, each contributing to my idea of what god asked of me and required of me.

Further, my god construct embraced qualities that I had difficulty in defending. I believed god was all loving and this made it extremely difficult to continuously explain the evil in the world and the tragic suffering of many of my parishioners.[91] I believed god was all knowing and that no individual or country or nation had an inside position or was somehow favored over other individuals, countries, or nations. (Today, in twenty-first century America, the belief in American exceptionalism is still promoted, i.e., the belief that the United States of America has been chosen by god to be an

---

91 This is the issue of *theodicy*, the problem of evil within the framework of a loving and caring god.

exceptional power and force in the governance of the modern world. I believed god was a god of all nations yet I encountered people in the churches I served who claimed that god especially favored the United States. I believed god was all powerful but I was frequently disappointed at the manner in which he (Yes, he! In those days we were not liberated from sexist language) refused to exercise power. I believed god answered prayer, at least once in a while, with a positive response. Mentors and ministerial colleagues would tell me either that I expected too much or that my faith was weak. In either case, the implication was that it was my fault, not god's.

The epigraph that opens this book essentially highlights the question of evil if one believes in an omnipotent and benevolent god. The quotation allegedly comes from Epicurus. (I have chosen the version passed down to us by David Hume.) What I am getting at is that my god construct was full of contradictions. Either god was not performing according to how I had been taught he does — or perhaps there was no god at all! Perhaps my idea of god that slowly grew into my personal god construct was nothing but an adult fairytale, or a figment of my wishful imagination? I still remember the first time I dared to entertain the thought that there was no such thing as god. I broke out in a total body sweat and I felt nauseous. Yet the thought persisted, "Could it be?"

I think my view of god changed drastically toward the negative side when I allowed myself to feel the full import of historical events where national leaders, for example, committed large-scale slaughter of whole categories of people, often including groups of their own citizens, and other horrors, from the European slaughter of native peoples around the globe to the Holocaust. And then there was the role the U.S. has played in the world, with Korea and Viet Nam and Serbia and Kosovo and Somalia and the Sudan and Darfur. Add to that 9/11, terrorism, Iraq, Afghanistan, the Taliban, Syria, Iran, and again Afghanistan and the Taliban. My construct of god had been based on a childlike faith. I lived almost four decades before I acquired the courage to let the god business go. And sometimes I find myself still doing mop-up work! And other times I ask myself how could I have been so naive to have created this construct?

Your God Construct

Again we come full circle to the question: What was your god-construct like? Are you clear about all the details of the god you don't believe in? What was your experience with your perception or your idea of god? Was your construct similar to mine or was your god more punishing and vindictive? Was your god a loving, forgiving father figure, or was your god a moral policeman following you around and checking on your daily roster of transgressions and sins? Was your god an authoritative avuncular figure who constantly prodded you on to a higher level of moral perfection? Are you completely rid of the sense of guilt that is often ground into those of us who fall short of the god-mark and fail to please the perfect god idol? Are you one of those unfortunate victims of parents and religious institutions who teach about punishment in the hereafter, threatening you with eternal damnation in the hell-fire of eternal torture?

If we are focusing on the meaningful constructs of life, we could also talk about your marriage construct or your family construct. Many people have an idealized construct of love and romance, especially as these play out in terms of sexuality. We could also consider your vocation and how your construct of meaningful employment has been fulfilling or disappointing, worthwhile or without reward, except perhaps for a pay check.

Be Your Constructs

What we usually refer to as our morals or our sense of morality is a functional application of our personal ethics. How we choose to behave is the result of what we believe. The evolution and development of these beliefs have resulted in constructs which give meaning to our existence. The most meaningful personal ethic that I have been able to construct for myself is an ethic of self-responsibility wherein I attempt to be what I am.[92] And what is that? To be myself or to be what I am is to be my constructs, to live out from day to day the implications of responsible personhood. This implies being faithful to myself; being faithful to my friends as well as to strangers; holding all life as being of infinite worth and value; being trustworthy in the eyes of others; being sensitive and accepting of those who would oppose me or otherwise put me down — while not necessarily approving or supporting their views or lifestyle, either.

Being my construct means to me that I accept my life as a gift from my parents within the realm and domain of nature. While I have a sense of gratitude for the opportunity of life, I am not grateful to any god or other supernatural force, i.e., beholden to any force beyond this life and this world. Nor am I beholden to my parents who sacrificed for me and saw a measure of their life's meaning in nurturing, socializing, and educating my sister, my brother, and myself. In the movie *Guess Who's Coming to Dinner*, the father of the lead male is scourging his son (Sidney Poitier) by describing the 75,000 miles he has walked as a postman, sacrificing for his son's future. The son then says to his father, "Let me tell you something. I owe you nothing. You did what you were supposed to do because you brought me into this world, and from that day you owed me

---

92John F. Crosby. *The Flipside of Godspeak: Theism As Constructed Reality.* Eugene, Oregon: Wipf and Stock. 2007. p. (See pages 72-75 for a discussion of the ethic of Eudaemonism — well-being.)

everything you could ever do for me. Like I will owe my son, if I ever have another."[93]

In the aftermath of trusting in a personal god, we are thrown back on our own resources. In the words of Ernest Becker, "When (mankind) dethroned the ideas of soul and God, he was thrown back hopelessly on his own resources, on himself and those few around him."[94] I agree with Becker that we are thrown back on our own resources, but I disagree that this is a hopeless situation. To the contrary, I see the dethronement of god as the greatest hope for humankind. I believe that only when god dies do we have a fighting chance to mature and grow up. When all gods die, perhaps we can then sit down and reason together about how to share planet earth without killing each other and enslaving nations and races and peoples. When all gods die, perhaps we will at last be able to share the blessings of nature and the challenges of human existence without destroying one another in the name of Yahweh, Allah, and God.

---

93 *Guess Who's Coming To Dinner*. Hollywood, CA.: Columbia Pictures Corporation. A Stanley Kramer Production.1967.

94 Ernest Becker. *The Denial of Death*. New York: The Free Press, 1973. p.190.

Chapter 8. Constructing Reality

"Epistem-what?" my masters degree student asked me. "Why can't you professors speak English?"

I replied: "O.K. Just answer this question. How do you know what you think you know?"

Epistemology

Epistemology is the study of how we come about knowledge. In a very real sense, epistemological questions are the most basic of all philosophical questions simply because until the epistemological questions are answered how can we begin to know what is true? To my dear student who wondered why I couldn't speak in English, I must address a series of questions.

1. How do we generate knowledge?

2. Do we rely on some authority?

3. If we do rely on authority, what qualifications must an authority have?

4. Is intuition a trustworthy and valid source of knowledge?

5. What is meant by revelation? Or revealed authority?

6. Is consensus a trustworthy authority?

7. Is personal experience a valid source of authority?

8. What if the experience is a personal revelation from god?

9. Is pragmatism, i.e., what works, a valid source of authority?

10. Is reason a valid source of authority?

11. Is empirical data a valid source of authority?

The problem with authority is the question: "Who (or what) says so?" The answers to the above questions are the stuff of epistemological inquiry. For example, I may trust my personal experience on many matters but I will turn to explicit theories in textbooks and journal articles for guidance on matters dealing with quantum physics, chemistry, climate change, evolution, human development, and all manner of engineering. If I desire answers to medical questions I will consult the best medical authorities, be they specialists or highly respected medical journals. Further, if I wish to find out which computers or automobiles have the highest reliability ratings I will go to the professional literature. To find out the most sound and otherwise advantageous place into which I should invest my savings I may go to several different authorities, just to do a cross check as to what is best for a person in my situation.

What Is Truth?

The question of truth is a part of the question of authority because alleged truth often depends on an authoritative source. There are several theories of truth that need to be briefly mentioned. First, and by far the most widely used, is the correspondence theory which says that for a belief to be true it must correspond with reality, i.e., the facts of reality. If you and I disagree as to which team won last year's Super Bowl, all we need to do to establish truth is to consult the records. Likewise, if I ask, "What is the truth regarding the effect of high blood pressure on the likelihood of stroke or heart attack?" all we need do is consult the reputable and authoritative medical literature. In other words, does our projected claim to truth correspond to reality?

Second, the coherence theory of truth holds that theories and hypotheses must be coherent with other theories or hypotheses. When at least two or more apparently valid theories regarding some facet of reality are congruent with one another, i.e., not in conflict, there may be a reasonable expectation of tentative truth. When we ask a question such as, "What is the truth about the origins of the universe?" we cannot appeal to correspondence. We must, instead, compare various theories regarding the origins of matter, of space, and of time. The data regarding the *Higgs boson* will be compared to other existing theory as to its degree of coherence or non-coherence.[95]

This is the heart of the issue regarding the conflict between the so-called creationism (or intelligent design) concept of truth and the theory of evolution. These two explanations for the origin or conception of the universe are emphatically not coherent. The intelligent design theory has no valid and authoritative science to back up its claims for truth. It has only conjecture and faith. The theory of evolution has come about as the result of many separate hypotheses regarding hundreds of species. Evolution adheres to a strictly scientific mode wherein nothing is absolutely final and all propositions are

---

95 As confirmed by research conducted at the Hadron Collider at the CERN laboratory (European Organization for Nuclear Research), near Geneva, Switzerland, in July of 2012.

pen-ultimate, never written in stone. The coherence theory of truth necessarily holds that all propositions and hypotheses must be *falsifiable*. This is to say that these propositions and hypotheses are always subject to rejection, revision, and further elaboration. "The key difference between coherence and correspondence is that coherence deals with the consistency of propositions and hypotheses in their agreement with each other, whereas correspondence deals with a consistency of events or propositions in their agreement with what is conceived as being reality."[96]

A third theory of truth is consensus. Consensus is dangerous in that it is based on public opinion and public belief. Simply put, if ninety-nine percent of Americans believe in a monotheistic god does this ensure the existence of such a god? A fourth test of truth is the test of pragmatism. Does what we believe have any utility? Does it work?[97]

First Order Truth and Second Order Truth

In order to establish a firm basis for this discussion, I would like to propose that there are two kinds of truth, First Order Truth and Second Order Truth. First Order truth is personal truth. It is your truth that you have come by and in which you believe. Whether it is truth about you or about your views of life or your views of how the universe came to be, first order truth is your truth. I may disagree with you and you may think my truth is crazy. Nevertheless, my truth is mine and yours is yours. To the extent that human beings can honestly agree on various propositions we may find consensus in the beliefs we hold as true. If human experience throughout many ages and encompassing almost all cultures and ethnic nationalities can come to a consensus that killing

96 John F. Crosby. *The Flipside of Godspeak: Theism As Constructed Reality.* Eugene, Oregon: Wipf & Stock. 2007. p. 31.
97 Ibid. Chapter Three, "The Quest For Truth".

and violence is wrong, we then would have a valid claim regarding authority. Even with a valid claim to authority, however, our truth about killing and violence is first order truth. This means it is true for us and until we have further information discrediting this truth we will continue to hold it as first order personal truth.

The older I get and the more times I go around the block, the more I am convinced that people will believe what they will believe, regardless of definitions of truth or criteria for truth. This is why I call first order truth personal truth. If your truth is true for you, then it is true — for you. That is why I call it first order truth.

Second order truth refers to beliefs and propositions regarding *ultimate* reality. As such, second order truth may never be known. Oh yes, some people think that they have a corner on second order truth, that is, they elevate or promote their first order truth into second order status by some sort of personal fiat. This is precisely the problem of religion in our world today. In the name of personal first order truth there are entire nations and religious cultures who are prepared to sacrifice their lives for their belief that their first order personal truth is, in fact, identical with universal second order truth.

I can only speculate about the nature of what I am calling reality because ultimate reality is unknowable in any final and objective sense of the word. Elsewhere I have stated, "As a constructivist, I do not believe that ultimate reality (or any other approximate synonym) is knowable. As close as I can come to objective reality is my belief in and acceptance of the subjective creations, inventions, and constructs of my own mind."[98] Von Glasersfeld says, "...knowledge does not constitute a 'picture' of the world. It does not represent the world at all — it comprises action schemes, concepts, and thoughts, and it distinguishes the ones that are considered advanta-

---

98Ibid., p. 38.

geous from those that are not. In other words, it pertains to the ways and means the cognizing subject has conceptually evolved in order to fit into the world as he or she experiences it."[99] When it comes down to the nature of ultimate reality, there is no possibility of absolute or firm knowledge. Of course, there are increasing degrees and levels of knowledge but all scientific research is subject to further hypothesis testing. If it is true science it must be falsifiable, i.e., it must be amenable to continuous research. Second order truth is what Immanuel Kant labeled as the *noumena*. Final and absolute truth of the second order, the noumena, is impossible.[100]

I hold that there are no exceptions to our human inability to actually know what I have labeled as second order truth. All that we can know about ultimate reality is our personal beliefs which are exclusively first order truth. All of humankind's various beliefs concerning ultimate reality fall under the category of first-order truth. This is where radical constructivism may help us see more clearly just how, and perhaps why, each of us who once believed in a personal god came to that belief. To bolster our own personal emotional security, because it is difficult to live with ambiguity, we claim that our personal first order god construct is the way things really are. And so we believe our construct. Our god construct becomes our first order truth and then we make the further unwarranted assumption that our first order construct is, in truth, identical to second order truth, demanding that everyone else in the world agree to accept it as such.

---

99 Ernst von Glasersfeld. *Radical Constructivism: A Way of Knowing and Learning.* New York; RoutledgeFalmer. 1995. p.114.
100 The only exceptions that both Immanuel Kant and Ernst vonGlasersfeld allow for the ultimate and final validity of knowledge regarding second order truth is in the area of mathematics and logic wherein a-prori premises are unassailable.

Radical Constructivism

Radical constructivism, in its more recent resurgence, goes back to Giambattista Vico.[101] Vico, writing prior to 1710, declared, "For the Latins, *verum* (the true) and *factum* (what is made) are interchangeable, or to use the customary language of the Schools, they are convertible...*The true is precisely what is made*"[102] (italics added). Ernst von Glasersfeld says of Vico, "As far as I know, Vico was the first to state unequivocally that our rational knowledge is constructed by ourselves."[103] Von Glasersfeld calls Vico the "first true constructivist."[104] Truth is what is made. Truth is what is created.[105]

Radical Constructivism is that branch of constructivism that claims that *reality* is the creation of the individual. In short this means that each of us perceives the world and all reality through our own eyes and our experience of perceiving leads us to invent or create our own reality. This is why Vico says that truth is what is made. Or, in other words, truth is in what we create. George Berkeley, the famous Irish philosopher and the second of the so-called 'British empiricists', (John Locke, George Berkeley, and David Hume), used the phrase *esse est percipi,* to be is to be perceived.

Constructivists do not deny that there is an independent reality out there and up there and all around us. But constructivists hold fast to the idea that humankind can only approximate this reality through the intermediary apparatus and

---

101 There are three main branches or divisions in modern constructivism. In addition to radical constructivism there is Personal Construct Psychology plus a third branch, reflecting social psychology, which deliberately uses the word, *constructionism* instead of constructivism.

102 Giambattista Vico. *On The Most Ancient Wisdom of The Italians: Unearthed from The Origins of the Latin Language.* 1710. Translated with an introduction and notes by L. M. Palmer, Ithaca and London: Cornell University Press, 1988. p. 45-46.

103 Ernst von Glasersfeld. *Radical Constructivism: A Way of Knowing and Learning.* New York: Routledger/Falmer. 1995. p. 37.

104 Ernst von Glasersfeld. "An Introduction to Radical Constructivism". In Paul Watzlawick,(Editor) *The Invented Reality: How Do We Know What We Believe We Know?* New York: W. W. Norton & Company. 1984. p.17.

105 Giambattista Vico. op. cit., p. 45-46.

processes of the mind. Only the mind, gathering data from the senses and based on the experience of living, can process the data, reflect on it, and thus come to some conclusion as to what it believes it perceives and experiences. Thus, the human mind is the inventor, creator, and the agency that constructs reality. This is not to say that in some future time the body of knowledge regarding the origin of the universe will not be accessible. Nevertheless, until such a breakthrough is firmly established all theory must remain theory. Physicists and astronomers, as well as scholars and scientists of related disciplines are involved in ongoing research. Perhaps one day there will be firmly established ultimate knowledge. But until that day, all alleged final or ultimate truth must remain conjectural and tentative.

Elsewhere I have written that theism and the god of theism is the result of constructivist thought.[106] This includes all of our religious and theological beliefs, regardless of how we came about these beliefs. Theologians of various persuasion came to their beliefs through the medium of sacred scripture, be it Christian, Talmudic, or Islamic. Others believe this scripture to be a direct revelation of a theistic god. Still others believe a god has spoken directly to them. Then there are those who claim they "feel" called of god. Many claim that their intuition and/or sixth sense is proof enough of the existence of god. Within Christendom there is appeal to the metaphysical beliefs of theologians such as St. Augustine, St. Thomas, and St. Anselm, as well as philosophers such as Aristotle, Descartes, and Kant.

Thinkers of all descriptions, including philosophers such as Plato, Aristotle, Descartes, Vico, Locke, Berkeley, Hume, and Kant have arrived at their own truth via the use of human reasoning based on one of two premises. The first of these premises is that we can know reality by way of inductive reasoning and logic, using our minds to reason our way into the

---

106 Crosby, op. cit., *The Flipside of Godspeak: Theism As Constructed Reality.*

nature of ultimacy and ultimate reality. This is called *ratio-nalism*. This method of reasoning is based on the assumption that the human mind is capable of making *a-priori* premises or statements which are *not* based on experience. (Immanuel Kant, in his *Critique of Pure Reason*, is perhaps the prime example of rationalist thought.)

The second of these premises is that we can only know reality by way of the mind reflecting upon and processing the data that comes to the individual through the senses and the experiences of life. This involves mental processing and reflection which we may label as human reasoning, but it is not to be called rationalism. It is called *empiricism*. Empiricism is always based on experience and is thus labeled as *a-posteriori*.

Radical constructivism rejects the first of these two alternatives. Radical constructivism is empiricist in its origins and is distrustful of premises that cannot be validated by the collected wisdom of human experience or by controlled scientific investigation and experimentation. Radical constructivism does not attempt to prove a negative, i.e., that there is *no* god up there or out there. The burden of such proof is not upon those of us who deny that god exists. Rather, it is always upon those who wish to prove that their perception of god does exist. And to do this they must substitute faith for knowledge. This entails, as we have seen, the use of an authority that does not pass the epistemological test, i.e., the test of answering the question, "How do we know?" Radical constructivism simply says that so-called ontological and metaphysical realities are beyond the pale of human existence. The radical constructivist accepts as fact that theological epistemology is an impossibility, i.e., that whatever constitutes ultimacy can never be known as second order truth, but rather only as first-order conjecture and speculation, which I have labeled as first order, personal truth. Von Glasersfeld concludes: "It may be useful to repeat that this is not a denial of reality...but it does deny that the human knower can come to know reality in the ontological sense."[107]

I would like to highlight two observations about how radical constructivism approaches the question of reality and human experience. *First, we, as the ones who observe reality, always become part of what we observe.* There is no such thing as pure objectivity, even for those of us who think we are being objective. The observer becomes part of the observed. The poet becomes part of his or her poetry. The pundit becomes part of the essay. The reporter part of what is reported. The therapist becomes part of the world of the observed client. The medic becomes part of the patient's world. The baseball umpire calls balls and strikes with no more and no less certainty than the professor who grades an essay. Even a researcher can become part of the experiment by way of the wording and phrasing of the several hypotheses. Needless to say, opinion pollsters are experts at phrasing questions that appear to be objective but in fact are worded so that the respondent is induced to answer in a given way.

The second observation about how radical constructivism approaches the question of reality and human experience is this: *believing is seeing.* We are most accustomed to the obvious reverse of the phrase, "seeing is believing." I do not dispute that seeing is oftentimes believing. Nevertheless, in a very real sense the reverse is also true: believing is seeing, because much of what we think we see depends on what we believe we saw and upon our will to believe. (According to popular belief, it was Yogi Berra who said, "If I hadn't believed it, I wouldn't have seen it," but Marshall McLuhan was first.) Belief oftentimes depends on our expectations. Belief sometimes depends on a mindset. Here is where the illusionist is in her or his prime. The illusionist creates belief. If one is not properly prepared for the illusion, then one does not see.

---

107 Ibid. p. 137.

I ask you, the reader, have you ever taken a drug prescribed for you by a physician? Most likely you have. What beliefs did you have about the ability of that prescription to help you in your medical distress? The point is that belief on the part of the patient is absolutely crucial to the practice of medicine. This has been proven in medical research tests where one group of patients is given the medication and another group is given a *placebo*, a benign sugar pill that has no healing value in itself. The patient or the research subject does not know which of the groups she or he is in, i.e., the experimental group or the control group. All of them are led to believe that they are given the real medication, and that the prescribed drug or procedure is going to remedy their ailment. Under such carefully controlled conditions it frequently happens that the control group using a placebo pill shows as much improvement as the other group. Why? Believing is seeing! The will to believe is a powerful influence upon what we believe to be the truth. The will to believe is a powerful influence upon what we perceive to be reality. A seminary professor of homiletics once said to me that the most important part of his job was to create a climate in which people were expectant in their faith, thus enabling them to see what otherwise they would not see.

And so it is amongst philosophers and psychologists, and dare we say, theologians. The backbone of the reality which we think we perceive is our wish that the reality be true. And believing that the reality is true, we invest ourselves in the reality to such an extent that the reality becomes truth, much as Vico's *verum factum* principle states: *truth is made*, truth is created or constructed. In an earlier writing I described how I constructed god and my faith in god. It was both my perception of god and simultaneously my belief in this god that enabled me to construct god. This process was no different than my perception of Santa Claus and my simultaneous belief in Santa Claus that enabled me to construct Santa Claus.[108]

Reconstructing and Constructing Reality

As I said in Chapter 2, you likely would not be reading this book if you were a comfortable and untroubled theistic believer. Something has happened to you that has caused you either to have a severe case of the doubts or has driven you away from theism altogether. This is probably one of the best things that ever happened to you, because it is giving you the opportunity to give birth to yourself, a daily challenge that I take very seriously and I hope you do also. I hold to a man-tra that continues to be personally meaningful to me. It is a line from the poem, *Faust*: "Yes! to this thought I hold with firm persistence; The last result of wisdom stamps it true; *He only earns his freedom and existence Who daily conquers them anew* "[109] (italics added).

You have within your power the ongoing ability to con-struct and reconstruct your entire life, your attitudes, your beliefs, and your values. I want you to pause and consider your past by asking two questions. First, how did I come to believe in the theistic god in the first place? How did I par-ticipate in the nurturance of this belief? (In other words, can you, will you, look into your past and attempt to determine precisely how your god belief was originally constructed?) Secondly, following this, How did I expand the original con-struct? How did I grow it, nurture it, and allow it to take firm root in my thinking? How did I continue to construct my god belief?

Perhaps these questions will trigger your thinking.

- What are my earliest images and ideas about god?
- From whom or where did they come?

108 Crosby, op. cit., *The Flipside of Godspeak: Theism As Constructed Reality. Appendix One.*
109 Goethe. *Faust.* Part II Act V Scene 6. (11575)

- Did my parents or parent take me to a church, synagogue, or mosque?

- Did my parents go with me or was I dropped off for some kind of educational program?

- Was my family regular at services or somewhat sporadic?

- Was I baptized or Christened or dedicated to god in any way?

- Did I attend a parochial school or a week-day religious school?

- Did my parents pray or say grace or invoke a blessing at meals?

- Was god connected somehow with me being admonished to be a good boy or good girl?

- Was divine punishment a part of my religious education?

- What was I taught about death?

- Was a belief in heaven and/or hell part of my religious upbringing?

- Was there much reference to the devil or to hell in my religious training?

- Did I ever have to memorize books of the Bible or passages from the Quran?

- Was I taught a catechism or creed or confession of faith?

- Did I go through a confirmation or rite of first communion or joining? Or a bar mitzbah?

- Was god and punishment for sin a theme of my early training?

- When I became sexually mature, did I feel guilty about thoughts of sex?

- Did I feel guilty (males) about having wet dreams? Or sexual fantasies and dreams?

- In my family was I free to ask questions about god, death, sin, punishment, and sex?

- When I asked questions, was I given straight answers or was I hushed up?

- When I left home to live apart from my family, did I continue to go to religious services?

- If I ever drifted away from god and the religious scene, did I ever attempt to come back? Why? When? Under what circumstances?

- Can I recall a time or circumstance when I identified religion or religiosity with the concept of meaning in life? (Please elaborate.)

- Have I struggled with issues such as evolution versus creationism, abortion versus putting the child up for adoption, the rhythm method of birth control versus contraception?

- Have I ever felt guilt about the way I have lived my life? About things I've done or failed to do?

- Since drifting away or breaking away from my belief and faith in god, have I felt forlorn or depressed or that my life was somehow meaningless or empty?

- Do I feel guilty when I think for myself, reflect critically, and otherwise question authority?

Von Glasersfeld has warned us: "... for constructivists, all communication and all understanding are a matter of interpretive construction on the part of the experiencing subject... "[110] We must never forget that we are the experiencing subjects von Glasersfeld is talking about. I hope that by now you are beginning to identify with what I mean when I talk about constructing your own faith. While you have had a lot of help in constructing your belief system, from family, the community, and the wider social order, it is also true that you yourself have played a big hand in the development of your god beliefs. In many and diverse ways, you have been the "heavy" in your own personal evolution. This is simply due to the fact

110 Ernst von Glasersfeld. "An Introduction to Radical Constructivism." In Paul Watzlawick, *The Invented Reality: How Do We Know What We Believe We Know?* New York: W. W. Norton, 1984. Part I Chapter I. p. 19.

that you internalized these beliefs. While you began the con-structing and internalizing processes long before you reached your so-called age of reason, the fact remains that you prob-ably never learned to think for yourself, at least not in any critical, assertive, or aggressive sense.

Perhaps it was fear that kept you guarded and afraid to ask questions. Perhaps it was fear of your parents, your priest, minister, or imam? Perhaps it was fear of punishment and/or the idea of eternal damnation in hell? Perhaps it was a fear of losing some sort of magic helper or divine puppeteer? Or perhaps it was fear that without god your life would be meaningless, worthless, and empty? In the last chapter we dwelt on the power of belief to guide our behavior. We at-tempted to look carefully at the process each of us experi-enced in our constructing of faith. By doing this we did what must be done before we are free to rebuild and re-construct. We tore down the edifice we consciously and unconsciously built. We cleared the land and now we are ready to start over by making a new beginning.

In the aftermath, you are free to become a reasoning and critical adult who has made the decision to disbelieve the re-ligious dogma of your past. You now realize that you, and you alone, are the agent who must challenge your former beliefs. You now see clearly how you constructed the faith that held you captive. You are now faced with abundant opportunity to create new foundations upon which you can construct the remaining years of your life. You now see clearly how your be-liefs play into the many constructs which in turn determine your future life course.

Chapter 9. Ethics

Over the years I have talked to many sincere non-believers who have shared with me their concern about what people would say to them if they admitted they didn't believe in god. Their concern centered upon the question of morality and motivation to lead a good life.

In what follows I endeavor to create a broad outline of an ethic rooted entirely within the natural order rather than the supernatural. The authority upon which this ethic is constructed is not without problems and questions. However, in the aftermath following the loss of god, I believe it to be far superior to an ethic based on a juvenile theism, an omniscient moral police god, or upon the preachments of the Santa Claus/Kris Kringle fantasy.

Prior to consideration of values and meaning in Chapter 10, we must frame a response to the question that apparently strikes at the heart of many who continue to cling to an idea of god as being the foundation for morality and ethics. Simply put, can we be good without god? Or, more productively, how can we be good without belief in god? When I speak to audiences, small groups, or to individuals, rarely, if ever, have

I not been faced with a retort, "Well, that's all well and good, but if there is no god, what motivation does anyone have for being good?" This response implies that without belief in god there would be no reason for human goodness, morality, or ethics, and that people would not be "good" if they didn't "have to." Even church goers have admitted to me that they don't actually believe the doctrine of justification by faith, or the idea of atonement for sin, or even the minister's sermons. I would always ask: "Then why do you participate in worship?" Invariably the answer is, "For the kids. They need to learn morality and we have to set an example."

I have been involved in many male-only discussions wherein the most common reply to the question of goodness and god is what I call the "no god – no fidelity" response, indicating that without a god who punishes transgressions, anything goes, especially sexual license. Responses like these indicate that many people believe that without god there would be no reason for sexual fidelity, for not cheating on your income tax, for not cheating on any kind of business transaction, or for trusting anyone, even your best friend. There would be no reason for professing a "moral" ethic simply because there would be, in their view, no accountability. People who feel this way seem to base their view on their understanding of the Bible, at least most Christians do. According to this view, accountability is an accountability to god, the ultimate judge and bookkeeper, and secondarily, if at all, to one's fellow human beings. This appears to me to be a shallow belief because it posits god as the one who is transgressed against rather than one's fellows, be they neighbors, adversaries, enemies, employers, employees, husbands, wives, sons, daughters, mothers, fathers, sisters, or brothers.

Philosopher Elizabeth Anderson believes the greatest opposition to evolutionary theory is not based on scientific theory but on moral theory. Her reasoning goes like this: "First, the fundamental religious objection to the theory of evolution is not scientific but moral. Evolutionary theory must be opposed (according to the fundamentalists) because it leads to rampant immorality, on both the personal and political scales. Second, the basic cause of this immorality is atheism. Evolutionary theory bears corrupt fruit because it is rooted in denial of the existence of God."[111] This raises the question, Is it true that people are actually afraid not to believe in god because they do not trust themselves? Is it true that all of us are filled with more evil impulses than good ones, and if there were no god to punish us in a hereafter, we would really allow our impulses to run rampant? Truly, if there is no god, will the human race descend into a pit of immorality akin to the biblical account of Sodom and Gomorrah? Will civilization crumble under the heavy burden of crime, greed, self-interest and a complete abandonment of responsibility to family, our society, and the world at large?

None of these fears is logical. People and civilizations have lived under various codes of morality from the dawn of civilization. The Code of Hammurabi (eighteenth century B.C.E.) and the Mosaic code (Moses probably lived in the thirteenth century B.C.E) are but compilations of the moral law that prevailed in those days. Even wandering tribes of hunters and gatherers did not wantonly kill humans without reason. If they did kill, it was usually a matter of territory and self-defense — kill or be killed — as a tribe attempted to secure and safeguard its food supply. Each tribe had its version of god or gods. Marriage rules of exogamy (without) and endogamy (within) the group evolved to govern whom one could or could not marry, discouraging marriage too close to one's own family tree and encouraging limited renewal of the gene pool (obviously, the exact science as to why this was necessary, and how it worked, would not have been entirely clear).

---

111 Elizabeth Anderson, "If God is Dead, Is Everything Permitted?" In, *the Portable Atheist: Essential Readings for the Nonbeliever*. Christopher Hitchens, (ed.), Philadelphia: De Capo Press (a member of the Perseus Books Group) 2007. Chapter 39, p. 333.

Even the commandment about adultery was based on an endogamous rule: the ancient Hebrew male could spread his sperm as he wished with non-Hebraic women: with Philistine women, Canaanite women, or women taken from other tribes captured in warfare; but he dared not get anything going with other Hebrew women, married or single. This would constitute adultery. The story explaining why this was important was that to do so would be to endanger the purity of the coming Messiah who must spring from the loins of a Hebrew woman who had been impregnated by an eligible Hebrew male. (Of course, this created a double standard as the Hebrew female could not have relations with anyone except her lawfully wedded husband.)

Other commandments such as the prohibition against killing, stealing, theft of property and bearing false witness were widespread in many early societies. These commandments or prohibitions had nothing to do with monotheistic belief but rather the practical need for communities of men and women to govern themselves and conduct their daily routines in an atmosphere conducive to peace and security. No tribe or community could survive without a strong measure of trust amongst its members. This trust, as we shall consider later, forms the basis for accountability to one's fellows.

The Question of Authority: Who or What Says So?

Ethics is a field of philosophy having to do with the foundation and rationale for human behavior and conduct. As such it often consists of a set of principles and premises of what is good and bad, desirable and undesirable, acceptable and unacceptable in both private and public transactions of individuals as well as corporate, political, and civic organizations. Ethics is considered to be the foundation of what is generally considered to be moral behavior and morality in general. In modern parlance the question is more often clothed in terms of morality and the idea of being good. Can we be good with-out god?[112]

In addressing the question of ethics without god, we be-gin with the question, Who says so? What says so? I maintain that the question of ethics is the question of authority. For the religious, i.e., the theistic religious, the authority is god. God has somehow revealed itself to humankind, especially to individuals who claim to have been embedded with the spirit of god. In doing so god has laid down the principles and laws, proscriptions and prescriptions, that humankind needs in or-der to live peacefully. These proscriptions and prescriptions include the indisputable fact that the Bible is full of direc-tives and dictates to mutilate, destroy, and massacre. Any fair and unbiased reading of the Old Testament and the reputed words of Jesus in the five gospels will reveal a multitude of horrible and repugnant verses relating episodes that are an affront to modern liberal believers and even to some evangeli-cal believers. [113]

Scholarship notwithstanding, the supreme authority for Jews, Christians, and Moslems is Yahweh, God, or Allah. De-fenders of this statement will claim that this authority and the teachings that result from belief in this authority are ab-solute. There can be no backing down, hedging, or fudging. One dare not ask about exceptions or errors in translation or even obvious contradictions. The sacred text is unalterable, inerrant, and literal. These devotees will ridicule, curse, and insult any and all who embrace the slightest degree of rela-tivity in terms of ethical codes and norms of behavior. Thus,

---

112 Greg Epstein, *Good Without God: What A Billion Nonreligious People Do Believe.* New York: Harper Collins, 2009.

113 Higher and Lower criticism of Matthew, Mark, Luke, and John yield the over-whelming likelihood these passages are the result of editorial redaction. Even the more liberal ministers appear reluctant to embrace this scholarship by challenging denominational creeds and by failing to share the fruits of biblical scholarship with their congregants, at least in their pulpits and public lectures. Many liberal clerics actually fear what would happen if they truly shared their seminary studies with their congregants.

abortion is utterly an offense that dare not be practiced even if the pregnancy is the result of rape or coercion. Historically, punishment for many offenses demanded shunning, stoning to death, and imprisonment.[114] The Inquisition stands as a monument to the terrible inflictions imposed upon anyone labeled, or even suspected of being, a heretic, dissenter, or non-believer.

In the aftermath of the end of faith in god, what authority do we have to direct and govern our behavior? Or, does anything go? If god is disqualified, then by what authority shall we live? Who or what will make the rules? Who or what will enforce the rules? If there are no absolute god-given prescriptions, directives, and commandments how shall humankind live together short of total anarchy?

Motivation in the Moral Behavior of Children

In the early 1970s a researcher by the name of Lawrence Kohlberg, building on the seminal work of Jean Piaget concerning the development of intelligence in children, posited three basic levels of moral development: the pre-conventional, the conventional, and the post-conventional. The pre-conventional consisted of two stages, stage one being the most basic of all motivations: obedience and punishment for disobedience. Stage two is the hope for reward. The importance of Kohlberg's research is that he highlights the notion that punishment and reward lie at the heart of childhood motivation. In other words, we learn fear at a very early age and with it we learn the expectation that we deserve to be rewarded when we are obedient.[115] Toddlers learn quickly that certain behaviors bring down the displeasure and wrath of a mother,

114 On this point and similar polemical propositions I refer the reader to authors such as Sam Harris, *The End of Faith*, W.W. Norton; Christopher Hitchens, *god is not great*, Twelve Press; Richard Dawkins, *The God Delusion*, Houghton-Mifflin; Dan Barker, *godless*, Ulysses Press.

115 Lawrence Kohlberg, *The Philosophy of Moral Development*. New York: Harper & Row, 1981.

father, or caretaker while obedience brings a feeling of approval and reward. There is an element of social exchange implicit in the punishment–reward transaction, i.e., if I do this you will do thus and so. "If I mind you, you will not punish me. Rather, you will reward me."

Kohlberg's level two, the conventional level, is based on stereotypic behavior of good boys and good girls in stage three, and law and order and conformity in stage four. Children learn quickly that certain social behaviors such as aggression and hostility drive potential friends away and that kindness and sharing usually attract reciprocal behavior.

Kohlberg's level three, the post conventional, advances to the social contract and to principled conscience in stages five and six.[116] Stage five includes social behavior which is deemed to be in line with the dictates, customs, and laws of the welfare of the greater community. Stage six of the post conventional level places us in a position of principled conscience wherein we behave in a selfless and altruistic manner for the greater good for the greatest number and for the general well being of the greater community and society. Total realization of stage six is an ideal stage which few actually attain on a day-in and day-out basis.

The importance of these stages cannot be overemphasized. People who believe in moral absolutes based on the god of their childhood and youth oftentimes spend their entire life living on Kohlberg's level one, the pre-conventional. They live their lives out of fear of punishment and in the steadfast belief that they will be rewarded by acceptance into the promised eternity of a kingdom in heaven. These are folks whose entire life is based on the premise that god is the source of all authority. These people will likely oppose the theory of evolution because it threatens their entire heaven-earth-hell three story cosmology. They are good people who believe that at death there will be a judgment concerning their private be-

116 Ibid.

havior — but not necessarily their corporate behavior and comportment. Some of these people sit on boards of directors of business and industry. Others are CEOs and serve as kings and queens of banking and financial institutions. As such, they do many things they would never do if they were acting as an individual. This is because when they are involved in a group, they do not feel they are responsible or accountable. This is also true of membership in organizations, clubs, and gangs.[117]

Kohlberg's treatment of the levels of moral development is certainly not the last word on the subject but it has served to bring research validity to the general theme of moral development in children. Carol Gilligan has challenged Kohlberg on the question of whether or not this research applies equally to females inasmuch as all of Kohlberg's research was done on male subjects. She claims that in the sequence of stages girls are more likely to be socialized into a stronger relationship ethos compared to boys, without the more rigorous emphasis on earlier punishment and rewards.[118]

The question remains: Do we carry into adulthood the most basic of our childhood fears and wishes as the basis for our judgments concerning both the elementary and the advanced moral issues facing humankind today? In other words, have we failed to outgrow and move beyond the early and rudimentary morality of early childhood? Do we remain at these early stages throughout our life, or do we search for an ethic grounded in accountability to one another and to society? If the ultimate authority is not the god of our infant image, a cosmological father that we have somehow transferred into the ultimate authority of personal right and wrong, then we must consider other possible sources of ethical authority. What would such an ethic look like?

---

117 See: Reinhold Niebuhr, *Moral Man and Immoral Society: A Study of Ethics and Politics.* New York: Charles Scribner's Sons, 1932.

118 Carol Gilligan, In *A Different Voice: Psychological Theory and Women's Development.* Cambridge, Mass. Harvard University Press, 1982.

The Golden Rule of Empathic Reciprocity

The golden rule is not considered authentic Jesus material, and it certainly did not originate with him. Quite possibly
it is was inserted into Jesus' teachings by New Testament re-
dactors, who edited this ancient aphorism. It appears as part
of the Sermon on the Mount (Matthew 7:12) and the sermon
on the plain (Luke 6:31), but according to The Jesus Seminar,
it is extremely unlikely this material is authentic.[119] It can be
found in negative form in the Tobit (4:15), "What you hate,
don't do to someone else." Rabbi Hillel, a Judean rabbi who is
reputed to have been a contemporary of Jesus, is supposed to
have said: "What you hate, don't do to another. That's the law
in a nutshell; everything else is commentary."

Quite apart from its historical origin, the golden rule, or
the rule of empathy and reciprocity, has survived the centuries as one of the most reliable keystones to moral and ethical
authority. It appears in one form or another in ancient texts
including Hindu texts, Buddhism, Taoism, and Zoroastrian-
ism. It was an important facet of the teachings of Confucius
and Laozi in ancient China, as well as in India, Egypt and
Greece.[120]

The chief criticism of the golden rule is the use of oneself
as prime referent, i.e., do unto others as you would have them
do to you. This reference appears to make oneself the norm
by which all others are to be treated? Does the golden rule
camouflage a calculating egoism? If so, then the golden rule
can hardly be accorded a place higher than level four in Kohlberg's taxonomy of stages because it places supreme value
on one's own welfare rather than the welfare of others. Of
course, it takes little imagination to change the rule to read:

---

119 Robert W. Funk and Roy W. Hoover, and the Jesus Seminar. op. cit., pp. 155-156.
120 For further amplification of the origins of the golden rule, see: Greg Epstein, *Good
   Without God: What A Billion Nonreligious People Do Believe.* New York: Harper Collins,
   2009, pp. 113.

Do unto others as you would have them do unto you and to all humankind.

Kant's Categorical Imperative

Kant's Groundwork of the Metaphysic of Morals deals with his views on the use of practical reason as compared to theoretical reason.[121] Some scholars consider the *Groundwork of the Metaphysics of Morals* (along with *The Critique of Practical Reason*) to be among the supreme moral-ethical critiques of all time, along with Plato's *Republic* and Aristotle's *Nicomachean Ethics*. *The Critique of Pure Reason* was Kant's supreme effort to disprove the ontological, cosmological, and teleological proofs for the existence of god. *The Critique of Pure Reason* illustrated the impossibility of knowledge concerning the ultimate, according to Kant's view. On the other hand, *The Critique of Practical Reason* was concerned with the basis for ethics and morality. Kant was attempting to isolate the ultimate authority for human behavior in terms of principles and rules for the living of everyday life.

In the *Groundwork of the Metaphysics of Morals* Kant formulated the categorical imperative, i.e., a formulation of one's duty framed in terms of what ought (the imperative) to be done in every situation, thus the universalization principle across all cultures and societies and situations. The category is the condition imposed, i.e., the un-conditionality of the demand. (An unconditional surrender is a categorical surrender in that there are no conditions or qualifications.) Kant very much wanted an absolute ethic which was both universal and unconditional. The categorical imperative rates a five or a six on the stage taxonomy of Lawrence Kohlberg, referred to earlier.

The first of Kant's two principles is the canon of universalization: Act only according to that maxim whereby you can,

121 Immanuel Kant, *Groundwork of the Metaphysics of Morals*. New York: Cambridge University Press, 1997. Immanuel Kant. 1724–1804. (Cambridge Texts in the History of Philosophy. Cambridge University Press.)

at the same time, will that it should become a universal law without contradiction.[122] The second principle is the principle of means versus ends: We should never act in such a way that we treat humanity, whether in ourselves or others, as a means only, but always as an end in itself.[123] We anticipate the principle of reciprocity because of our expectation that others will treat or deal with us in like manner.

In terms of accountability, we are justified in holding others accountable just as we are accountable to others. This is to say that others are justified in holding us accountable. If we hold ourselves as somehow exempt from accountability then we must hold others as also exempt from accountability. In short, the basis of an ethic of accountability is in its mutuality and universality.

Kant assumes that human behavior, in terms of ethics and morality, is born of free will. Without the premise of free will there would be no meaning or purpose to the question of ethics or morality. He recognizes that there are exceptions to the concept and reality of free will. There have always been situations wherein humankind is deprived of free will such as in prisoner of war situations or human slavery situations. However, even as a prisoner of war there may be meaningful examples of free will and autonomous behavior. Kant recognizes that without free will there can be no truly autonomous behavior and hence the entire concept of moral behavior would be meaningless.

The Sermon on the Mount and the Second Great Commandment

While I do not disparage the love ethic of Jesus as recorded in the Sermon on the Mount (Matthew 5: 1-7:28), I have great difficulty submitting all my personal, community, eco-

---

122 Ibid. Kant, p. 31. (4:421)
123 Ibid. Kant, p. 38. (4:429)

nomical, and political actions and behaviors to its dictates, preachments, and aphorisms. According to the Jesus Seminar, the Sermon on the Mount contains only a few sequences of interspersed authentic and nearly authentic Jesus material.[124] As we have seen, the golden rule is definitely not original Jesus material, even though it is contained in the Sermon on the Mount.

The reputed second great commandment of Jesus, "You are to love your neighbor as yourself," is a fine thought, but it does not rise above Kohlberg's stage four because the referent is not humankind but only the self. Further, it does not measure well on accountability. There continues to be considerable debate amongst New Testament scholars concerning whether this commandment came from Jesus or from the famous Jewish rabbi Hillel, a time cohort of Jesus.[125] Nevertheless, while the admonition to love others as we love ourselves is time honored and a wonderful ideal by which to base our human activity, it simply lacks the impetus to adjudicate amongst peoples who have honest differences as well as irreconcilable hatred and enmity toward one another.

The Canons

In the aftermath of my loss of god, I have settled on five canons of ethical behavior. These canons are not the last word or even the penultimate. It is possible to criticize them as not being perfect or as less than totally comprehensive. Nevertheless, they are valid in terms of construct validity, that is, the referent definitions of empathy, reciprocity, accountability, truthfulness, and universality, are sufficiently lucid and explanatory so as to characterize accurately what they purport to represent. They serve to encapsulate the meaning and es-

---

124 Robert W. Funk, Roy W. Hoover, and the Jesus Seminar. *The Five Gospels: The Search for the Authentic Words of Jesus.* New York: Polebridge Press, Macmillan Publishing Company, 1993. pp 139-158..

125 Ibid .Funk and Hoover. p. 237.

sence of an all-encompassing ethical system which will steer us through the personal, economic, political, and social dilemmas to which we are all subject. In turn, these five canons yield further principles and norms such as self- responsibility, honesty, equity, and equality.

Empathy. Without empathy it is almost impossible to feel into the situation of another. Merriam Webster defines empathy thusly:

1. Empathy is the imaginative projection of a subjective state into an object so that the object appears to be infused with it.

2. The action of understanding, being aware of, being sensitive to, and vicariously experiencing the feelings, thoughts, and experience of another of either the past or present without having the feelings, thoughts, and experience fully communicated in an objectively explicit manner.[126]

According to psychoanalyst Heinz Kohut, known for his work in Self Psychology, "Empathy is the capacity to think and feel oneself into the inner life of another person."[127] Empathy is not an exclusively human trait. The chimpanzee and the bonobo (*Pan paniscus*) show signs of behavior which may be properly labeled as empathic. The term is of relatively recent origin, having been credited to E. B. Tichenor in 1909.[128] It is worth noting that the golden rule, in whatever form, demands a healthy measure of empathy. If one lacks empathy, or the ability to feel into the situation of others, the golden rule loses its power to motivate behavior simply because the non-empathic person lacks a modicum of ability to "feel into" the plight or situation of another. It is not a coincidence that people without the ability to be empathic are a concern to the mental health community, simply because the non-empathic person is at a severe disadvantage to understand and appre-

126 *Merriam Webster's Collegiate Dictionary,* Eleventh Edition. Springfield, Massachusetts, 2003.
127 Wikipedia. http:en.wikipedia.org/wiki/Empathy
128 Ibid.

ciate the effect of her/his behavior, including body language and speech, on peers, colleagues, associates, and adversaries.

(It is well for us to remember that the word 'empathy' did not exist in Kant's time, nor indeed in any time prior to 1909. Nevertheless, the concept underlying the word was quite genuine.)

In terms of practical application, the school bully displays a lack of empathy for the person being bullied. Bullying in any form shows a lack of caring for another's welfare. A young man of 23 came to me for counseling, and related that since he was about seven years old, he'd had to wear very thick lenses in his glasses. This young man was no longer wearing thick glasses, but he has struggled for years because of the demeaning and cruel statements non-empathic people made to him in his youth. If these thoughtless people had had even a modicum of empathy they would not have made such statements, at least not to his face. When parents use put-down words and make demeaning comments to their children the message they impart can become a debilitating script and a curse in later life.

One of the most telling tests of mental health is one's ability to practice empathic listening and caring. Empathic ability or inability is one of the most important factors contributing to diagnosis on the autism spectrum. Indeed, our empathic ability is one of the traits that contribute to the civility of human life and distinguishes civilizations, one from another, in terms of the protection and safeguarding the general wellbeing.

Reciprocity. Reciprocation is the situation of paying one back in some form of balanced transaction. To reciprocate is to return the favor in an equitable manner. Merriam Webster states: To return in kind or degree; Reciprocate implies a mutual or equivalent exchange or a paying back of what one has received. A mutual exchange of privileges.[129] For our purposes

---

129 *Merriam Webster's Collegiate Dictionary, op. cit.*

reciprocation insists that all interactions and transactions, whether between individuals, groups, companies, corporations, or governments, be balanced and in equitable or fair exchange. Usually empathy stands close to reciprocity, or the wish and justifiable expectation that our colleague or adversary will respond to us in like manner. The golden rule literally cries out for reciprocation. "...as you would have others do unto you" is a reciprocal expectation. We first have empathy, the ability to feel into what we believe the other person is feeling. Secondly we reciprocate the feeling by altering our verbal or physical response in order to demonstrate that we have at least a modicum of understanding of what they are experiencing, i.e., we do unto them just as we hope and trust they would do to us if the tables were turned.

Accountability. For a person, business entity, enterprise, or corporation to be held accountable is, at face value, to be held responsible for its practices, behaviors, transactions, and interchanges. If there is no accountability there can be no civil or criminal law nor any personal or corporate responsibility for behavior, practices, and policy. As such, accountability is the legal cornerstone for civilized society and its systems of courts and jurisprudence.

The canon of accountability is inherently present in the formulation of the categorical imperative. When we choose to act in any given manner and in any given situation, we are thereby demonstrating our willingness that everyone else would be justified in doing what we now contemplate and that in so acting we are accountable for our decisions and actions.

Truth. The canon of truth or truthfulness must stand as a pre-requisite for a viable ethical code. Without truth there is no possibility for face to face interchanges, not to mention transactions in business, industry, diplomacy, and all manner of statecraft. In Chapter 8 we defined truth in several ways including the coherence theory, the correspondence theory, intuition theory, and the consensus theory. Suffice it to say that in practical matters the correspondence theory of truth is usually quite adequate in that it establishes a link between an activity or happenstance and our human account of the circumstances surrounding the activity or happenstance.

Universality. All ethical or moral principles apply to all others sharing the same class or sub-class. A guideline, norm, or principle must be equally applicable to all members of the class under consideration. There can be no exceptions or exclusions to the behavioral codes. If a norm of behavior or practice applies to one person it ought to apply to all persons. If it applies to one country it ought apply to all countries. If it applies to one defined entity it ought apply to all similar entities without exception. This principle applies to all races, ethnic backgrounds, differences in social and economic status, religions, and sexual/gender diversity.

Authority Again

Earlier I raised the question of authority as being the key question when it comes to a code of ethical behavior. Who says so? What says so? If it is not god "up there" and "out there" laying down the laws and proclaiming the commandments, then whom should we follow and to what directives should we hearken? Elizabeth Anderson summarizes the authority issue very succinctly: "We each have moral authority with respect to one another. This authority is, of course, not absolute. No one has the authority to order anyone else to blind obedience. Rather, each of us has the authority to make claims on others, to call upon people to heed our interests and concerns...I am arguing that morality as a system of reciprocal claim making, in which everyone is accountable to everyone else, does not need its authority underwritten by some higher, external authority. It is underwritten by the authority we all have to make claims on one another."[130]

Short of some form of divine revelation which I have completely rejected (Chapter 1), the question of the source of authority must come from within the confines of the history of our collective human experience. Perhaps this is as good as it can ever be ... or in modern parlance, perhaps this is as good as it gets. If so, so be it. Nevertheless, I challenge myself and all who would disavow a divine revelation of authority to live in the spirit of the canons of empathy, reciprocity, accountability, truthfulness, and universality.

In the aftermath of the loss of god, I am eager and willing to defend the ethic that I have herein outlined as more worthy of my human commitment than the so-called moral-ethical system based on portions of the Old and New Testament, i.e., even after the terrible atrocities and war killing stories are eliminated or expunged. I wish to reiterate that the five canons of the ethic I have proposed are rooted in the natural order without reference to the supernatural. This natural order includes the use of logic, reason, and as frequently as possible, a methodology based on the scientific method. Basically, these characteristics are the canons of historic humanism dating back to Epicurus, Lucretius, Erasmus, Hume, and Kant.

---

130 Elizabeth Anderson. op. cit. pp 346-347.

CHAPTER 10. VALUES AND MEANING

What is the meaning of human existence? I have taken half a lifetime to answer this question for myself. My answer came most clearly when I was reading Viktor Frankl's book, *Man's Search for Meaning*.[131] I will give my answer at the end of the chapter. First, I would like us to consider the relation be-tween values and meaning.

Value Creates Meaning

Put in simple terms, what we value in life is what gives meaning to life. Without the concept of value, there could be no such thing as meaning. Those of our possessions that we no longer value (or never did value), we ought to dispose of, if for no other reason than that they clutter up our busy lives. If we do not hold something, i.e., an object, a person, a dream, a goal to be of value, that object, person, dream or goal simply cannot be meaningful to us in any significant sense.

---

131 Viktor Frankl, 1959, 1963. *Man's Search For Meaning.* (Originally published as *From Death Camp to Existentialism*). Boston: Beacon Press. (Washington Square Press, Edition.1963. New York: Simon & Schuster)

This is what Viktor Frankl discovered during his imprisonment at Auschwitz. "As for myself, when I was taken to the concentration camp of Auschwitz, a manuscript of mine ready for publication was confiscated. Certainly, my deep concern to write this manuscript anew helped me to survive the rigors of the camp. For instance, when I fell ill with typhus fever I jotted down on little scraps of paper many notes intended to enable me to rewrite the manuscript, should I live to the day of liberation. I am sure that this reconstruction of my lost manuscript in the dark barracks of a Bavarian concentration camp assisted me in overcoming the danger of collapse."[132]

Frankl claims that it is not enough to have a general purpose in life. To have a general purpose or meaning in your life is fine as far as it goes, but it does not go far enough. We need specific goals, purposes, and meanings. We need, in the terms of the constructivists, to be creating, inventing, and constructing. As Vico says in his *verum factum*, truth is in what is made. Put in more pedestrian or vernacular terms, we were not made to sit around. The human body thrives on both physical and mental exercise. Our bodies decay and wilt when there is a lack of purposeful activity and endeavor.

Julian Young distinguishes two kinds of meaning in life. First is what he calls the "grand narrative." This refers to the overall and all encompassing meaning one's life may or may not have in terms of an eternal purpose or eternal meaning according to a plan of a theistic deity. Second, is the "personal narrative." The personal narrative is the practical, everyday, here-and-now meaning each of us may or may not give to his/her own existence.[133]

Frankl is far less concerned with the grand narrative than with the specific narrative. He is focused on the personal nar-

---

132 Ibid; p. 165.
133 Julian Young. *The Death of God and the Meaning of Life*. Routledge, Taylor & Francis Group, London and New York. 2003. p. 168 f.

rative. He states: "...[T]he meaning of life differs from man to man, from day to day and from hour to hour. What matters, therefore, is not the meaning of life in general but rather the specific meaning of a person's life at a given moment.... Everyone has his own specific vocation or mission in life; everyone must carry out a concrete assignment that demands fulfillment. Therein he cannot be replaced, nor can his life be repeated. Thus everyone's task is as unique as is his specific opportunity to implement it." [134]

Existence Precedes Essence

We must pause to consider one of the most basic axioms of *existentialism*. The basic question is the question of meaning in life and its correlate, the question of determination of the source of meaning. Theism of every description assigns god as the source of meaning in life. According to this way of thinking the godhead gives meaning to each and every human being who has ever lived. First comes meaning and secondly comes existence. Hence, *essence precedes existence*. Theists of all descriptions claim that god alone gives both ultimate and specific meaning to their life. In this sense, *essence* or meaning and significance of being, is a pre-given. The individual must now ponder the divine meaning of his or her existence and attempt to discern practical manifestations of this pre-given essence.

The existentialist says "no" to the theistic way of thinking. The existentialist simply confronts the fact of his or her existence. Here I am. I am alive, human, and unique. I have mental and physical powers and talents and abilities. I have been given a life and the only source of this gift is my human biological/physiological inheritance. Hence, my *existence precedes my essence*. My being alive and human precedes the meaning

---

134 Frankl, op. cit., p. 172. (Emphatically, this is the reason the author, John Crosby, has written this book.)

which I alone can give to my existence. No one else can do it for me. No parentage, no socio-cultural-financial inheritance, no god, no divine revelation. I am the responsible one. Me and only me. There is no other. I am the meaning maker. My essence is my responsibility.

Paul Tillich, referring to Jean-Paul Sartre, states that the single most powerful sentence in the literature of existentialism is "[Sartre's] proposition that 'the essence of man is his existence'. This sentence is like a flash of light which illuminates the whole Existentialist scene. One could call it the most despairing and the most courageous sentence in all Existentialist literature. What it says is that there is no essential nature of man, except in the one point that he can make of himself what he wants. Man creates what he is. ... Man is what he makes of himself. And the courage to be as oneself is the courage to make of oneself what one wants to be."[135]

Actualizing Values

The original title for Viktor Frankl's book which I quoted earlier was *From Death-Camp to Existentialism*. The existential reality is that we are the ones who are responsible for ourselves and our own existence. We are the thinking ones, the doing ones, the agents by which change can come about. We are the meaning makers and we are the meaning givers, first in terms of responsibility to ourselves to make something meaningful and significant of our life and second to give of ourselves in the enrichment of humanity and all life.

Frankl states: "Logotherapy deviates from psychoanalysis insofar as it considers man as a being whose main concern consists in fulfilling a meaning and in actualizing values,

---

135 Paul Tillich. *The Courage To Be*. New Haven: Yale University Press. 1952. pp. 149-150.

rather than in the mere gratification and satisfaction of drives and instincts..."[136]

What does it mean to actualize values? To me it means that values are not some nice thing people like to talk about, whether they are family values or human values, Democratic party values or Republican party values, liberal values or conservative values, progressive values or fundamentalist values. To actualize a value is to bring it to life. This means to implement the value, practice it, and live it.

At a recent presentation I mentioned the relationship between purposeful activity and meaning in life. A gentleman who was employed on the assembly line at a near-by plant raised his hand and asked me to be more specific. "Fair enough," I replied. My response went something like this: "Finding meaning on the assembly line is in doing one's particular job to the utmost of one's ability. Purpose and meaning come from thinking on the job regarding ways and means of performing the task better and with less energy output or with less stress. Meaning is also to be found in how one relates to fellow workers and to one's attention to listening instead of constantly talking or prescribing to others how they should deport themselves. There is value and consequent meaning in being innovative in the office, the work room, or the factory. Creating one's personal residential habitat can be extremely purposeful for the home landscaper, gardener, or carpenter."

I continued: "One of the sad things about modern life is that so many people have retirement as a goal but then do not know what to do with themselves when that day finally arrives. Purposeful activities, hobbies, and pastimes not only keep people active and interested and involved, they may also keep one's mind occupied and one's body reasonably mobile. Don't let people make fun of your volunteer work. Hospital work, prison work, library work, educational tutoring, and

---

136 Frankl, op. cit., p. 164.

all kinds of community work await the alive and aware. Being Big Sisters or Big Brothers and numerous educational challenges fill the days of many retirees."

There is an old scenario about a theologian and a graduate student observing three men among hundreds doing the stone work on a cathedral. "What are you doing?" the theologian asked one of the workman. "I am building a magnificent cathedral for the glory of God" was his proud response. Then the theologian said to the second laborer: "What are you doing?" The second laborer answered: "I am creating a wall of fine stone." The theologian asked the third craftsman the same question: "What are you doing?" to which the craftsman replied: "I am earning a day's wage to support my family." The theologian asked his student, "Which do you think is doing holy work?" The student paused for a few seconds before replying: "I believe," said the student, "that the man who answered that he was supporting his family was doing the holy work." Actually, all three were doing meaningful work, which by extrapolation could mean that all three were also doing holy work.

I am saying that, in the aftermath, we are in a unique position to see all of life as sacred and all of life as a treasured gift. One need not believe in a god in order to believe that life is sacred. Indeed, the very fact that life is short, that there is a beginning and an end, is the driving force behind the quest for meaning in life. If there were no end, there really could be no meaning to our existence. I remain steadfast in my belief that values give meaning to our existence, but only when these values are actualized and implemented.

Others have paved the way for you. Now it's your turn to pay forward.

Trisha

Ever since I first became acquainted with Viktor Frankl's *Logotherapy* I have been keenly aware of the vital importance of the sense of meaning and purpose a person experiences or fails to experience in daily life. Regardless of whether I was working with one or several clients in marital or family therapy, I always alerted myself to a possible sense of loss. The loss could be catastrophic, sudden, and irreplaceable such as a father, mother, husband, wife, child, or grandparent. Or it could be the loss of employment, of opportunity, of value, of meaning or any of the losses we discussed in Chapter Four.

I recall a married couple, Trisha and Lloyd. I had seen them in conjoint therapy for about five sessions some years ago when she was mired in a state of mild depression which was having a negative effect on their relationship. Lloyd owned a small tool and die business. Trisha had not worked outside the home since the children were born. Their two children, Jennifer and Joshua, were now grown and on their own. The situation improved, and when I last saw Trisha and Lloyd together as a couple they were coping well and were in a much better frame of mind. I did not see Trisha again for almost two years. She phoned one afternoon and asked for an appointment. She said she was very down — felt listless — low energy — depressed. She said Lloyd would not be coming. She just wanted to check in on a few things.

"I feel guilt. I cared for Mom until I had to put her in a home. I saw her every day until the day she died but she didn't know me. It was Alzheimer's. Since then I've been in a funk. My kids never came to visit their grandmother. They never did seem to show much interest in their grandparents. That still bothers me. They seem so self-centered. Lloyd's been very supportive. I think his work is his first love. But I just can't seem to get on top of things. Now that Mother's gone I feel like there's nothing left for me. Lloyd keeps busy at the shop and the kids have their own lives. I used to turn to God to give me strength but I don't think I even believe in God anymore."

I probed here and there and listened attentively to her complaints about her children. Most of her comments seemed to cluster around her feelings of guilt and her alleged sense of despair. Her guilt appeared to be the result of having to put her mother in a home and being unable to "be there for her" all the time. I worked with her about the situation and I attempted to challenge her interpretation of events. Trisha mentioned on several occasions that she felt she had let her mother down and that she was somewhat of a failure as a daughter. Her interpretation of her situation seemed to be a reflection of how she defined the role of a dutiful daughter. She perceived herself to be a failure. She had a severe and rigid mental construct of what a "good" daughter should be. I listened as she revealed her mental images and constructs, especially as to how she defined her duty toward her mother and things she wished she could have done differently. At every turn I focused on her self-definitions and interpretations.

At first, I set upon a course of listening to Trisha tell her tale. After the third session, I changed course a bit and became more active — more in the spirit of Frankl's *Logotherapy*. I have often reminded myself of Frankl's playful caricature of logotherapy. "During psychoanalysis, the patient must lie down on a couch and tell you things that sometimes are very disagreeable to tell...in logotherapy the patient may remain sitting erect, but he must hear things that sometimes are very disagreeable to hear."[137]

I attempted to help Trisha see and understand that in many and diverse ways she had in the past, and even more now in the present, done truly significant things for both her parents. I shared that I found a great deal of meaning and purpose in what she had done for her father and, most recently, her mother. Likewise, I attempted to help her see her and

137 Ibid. p. 152.

Lloyd's efforts in the raising and nurturing of their two children in a positive light. Painstakingly, and as unobtrusively as possible, I guided her to reconsider her values in life. I attempted to show her how these values made her life worthwhile and how there was meaning and purpose in all that she had done for her mother.

I was keenly aware that I dared not talk too much. I defined my role to be one of asking probing questions and gently guiding Trisha to redefine herself and to create a new life for herself. She talked about the meaning of love and how she never could share her parent's belief in a god and an afterlife. This seemed to me to be the heart of her feeling of guilt and despair, i.e., she simply couldn't live up to her parents' expectations, especially their expectations concerning Trisha's religious beliefs.

Then one day I simply confronted her. I told her that we would take four weeks off. In four weeks we would have our final session. I told her, point blank, that she did not need me and that as long as she had our therapy session to fall back upon, she would likely fail to become involved in meaningful and purposeful activity. "It's time," I said, "to give birth to a new Trisha who could be vibrant and alive and enthusiastic about many things, but it was up to her to explore and experiment and try out new activities and projects, new ways of being."

After our interval, at the session which I had said would be our last, she told me how bewildered and stunned she had felt at my presumptiveness in ending therapy. She confronted me by claiming that I had betrayed her. At this, I assured her that in the course of our previous therapy I had detected no neurosis and no personality disorder. I simply saw no reason for her to continue therapy. I shared my feeling that after the death of both her parents, she had been left with a feeling of emptiness, that she had found meaning in her commitment to her parents and that now she was experiencing a deep loss of purpose in her daily life. I assured her that I believed in her and that she had great potential, and that what was needed was for her to create a life wherein she could fulfill a vital role in the lives of others."[138]

I did not hear from her again, but one day, about a year or so later, I received an envelope in the mail. It contained a full page feature article about Trisha's pivotal role in the founding and development of a walk-in clinic for mothers who very much needed a short (morning or afternoon) break or respite from their young children. Attached to the article was a one-word note signed by her husband, Lloyd. "Thanks." Receiving the note and then reading the article put a smile on my face and gave me a sense of pride. I had taken a chance! I had refused to let her continue in a useless therapy exercise. In a sense, I had challenged her to go out and find a new purpose for her life, a new perspective, a new frame of reference for being. Is she still upset and angry with me for having ended her therapy? Maybe! Probably! But who cares? She found a purpose for her own life and she is making her life count.[139]

In the aftermath of the loss of god, we are left on our own to define and redefine, to create and recreate, to construct and reconstruct values, meaning, and purpose for ourselves. No one can ever do this for us. No teacher, therapist, guru, minister, priest, rabbi, or imam can possibly fulfill another's existence or redeem another's life. Here is my personal answer

---

138 Sheldon Kopp. *If You Meet the Buddha On the Road, Kill Him. The Pilgrimage of Psychotherapy Patients.* Palo Alto, CA.: Science and Behavior Books. 1972. "Once a patient realizes that he has no disease, and so can never be cured, he might as well terminate his treatment. He may have been put in touch with good things in himself, and may even still be benefiting from the relationship with the therapist, but once he realizes that he can continue as a disciple in psychotherapy forever, only then can he see the absurdity of remaining a patient, only then does he feel free to leave. We must each give up the master, without giving up the search." (Bantam Book Edition, p.188.)

139 This sounds a bit like Provocative therapy where the hoped for response by the client is: "Well, I'll show him!"

to the question I posed in the first paragraph of this chapter. What is the meaning of human existence? Five words: *Life is its own meaning.* Make of it what you will. Believe in yourself. Be your own construct. Trust your own judgment. Be your own authority. Always pay forward.

Afterthoughts

Thought One: In the aftermath, every single day becomes increasingly important, increasingly precious, and increasingly challenging. The reason for this is quite simple. With god's demise, the wish dream of hundreds of thousands of years is exposed for what it is, i.e., a wish. This dream has always pointed to immortality in some form of afterlife experience. Hardly a day goes by that I fail to read either an obituary or a letter-to-the-editor talking about someone going to live with her heavenly creator or going to be with the Lord. From my point of view, without such a belief in an imaginary afterlife, each day is a gem to be treasured and lived to the max. I realize that legions of devout believers take great comfort in their belief in a hereafter with reunions with loved ones. Nevertheless, for me, I must repeat what I said earlier: My heart will never accept what my mind rejects.

Thought Two: In the aftermath there is no pie-in-the-sky by and by, and there is no heavenly home where the good can dwell in some form of ethereal kingdom and the bad folks will be sent to the devil's office in the kingdom of hades or sheol or hell, sometimes known as the valley of Gehenna, the refuse and garbage pit outside Jerusalem. With god's demise comes the promise and the challenge of humankind's major purpose and goal — *to improve the human lot for all peoples of this earth.* To be rid of famine and debilitating disease; to be rid of useless and senseless killing; to be rid of suffering and pain of all kinds and descriptions; to be rid of sexual slavery and exploitation; to be rid of silly and counter- productive beliefs that deter humankind from pursuing peace and true humanity. Perhaps this translates into national and world governments that absolutely prevent man's and woman's exploitation of fellow humans.

Thought Three: The fact that you have read this book is very likely a sign that you are on the other side of the god question. That's a good thing because, as Becker says, "When you put all your eggs in one basket you must clutch that basket for dear life."[140] Perhaps, like me, you once put all your eggs in one basket. But you have grown up since then! You no longer need to clutch the god basket. You have come to realize, perhaps after a goodly amount of pain and suffering, that god is but the adult version of Santa Claus. Perhaps you have come to see that when people kill each other and maim each other for life, when they exploit each other, when they would rule over others, and even commit genocide in the name of the god they worship, then this god idea needs to be challenged more than ever before.

Thought Four: If you have never told your story or your tale to anybody, please purchase a notebook of some sort and begin writing your journal. In your journal, tell an imaginary reader who you are. As a beginning outline, you may wish to dwell, at least initially, on the chapter titles of this book. Talk about your primal fear and flesh out your philosophy of life and death. Tell your reader how you handle anxiety. Tell about your losses in life and how you have overcome them. Are you courageous? How did you learn to be courageous?

140 Ernest Becker, op. cit., p. 180.

Tell about yourself and how you have overcome the pseudo-self that tries to impress people. Introduce your solid self. Review your beliefs and attempt to determine just how each belief has become part of a construct that in turn determines how you live your life. How have you constructed your life? Do you see clearly what you have let others do to you and perhaps what you have done to others? Do you see what you have done to yourself and what needs to be reconstructed? Focus on each significant relationship including your mother, father, sons, daughters, in-laws and others. Lastly, look to your values and attempt to relate each significant value to the meaning you have given to your own existence.

Thought Five: For many of us, learning to live without god was not easy. It was like learning to look at the world, the universe, and all human life in a different light and in a different way. At first we took tiny, childlike, steps, and then slowly we began to walk with a secure stride. In the aftermath we began to see more clearly the mythological fairytale that had been laid upon us. And then we also began to learn and understand that no god, no teacher, no guru, no master, no imam, no priest, no minister, no rabbi, no therapist, no holy reincarnation from a by-gone era has the answers for your life. If any person or authority figure pretends to be your lord or master or your Buddha, then rise up and go forward — and "if you meet the Buddha on the road, kill him."[141]

Thought Six: I believe your life can be filled with a richness and purpose far greater than that promised by St. Paul, St. Augustine, St. Thomas, or any of the other Christian saints

---

141 Sheldon Kopp. *If You Meet the Buddha On the Road, Kill Him. The Pilgrimage of Psychotherapy Patients.* Palo Alto, CA.: Science and Behavior Books. 1972. (Bantam Book Edition, p.188.) "'If you meet the Buddha on the road, kill him!' This admonition points up that no meaning that comes from outside of ourselves is real. "'The Buddhahood of each of us has already been obtained. We need only recognize it. Philosophy, religion, patriotism, all are empty idols. The only meaning in our lives is what we each bring to them. Killing the Buddha on the road means destroying the hope that anything outside of ourselves can be our master. No one is any bigger than anyone else. There are no mothers or fathers for grown-ups, only sisters and brothers."

and church fathers. Human kind is now, and has been for centuries, under pressure to bow down to some sort of authority, be it the authority of Scripture, the Pope, the Church, or some other authority such as the Quran, the Book of Mormon, the Watchtower, the Readings of Christian Science, the popular guru or the modern-day version of the shamans known as psychotherapists. Once we have overthrown the terrible yoke of supernatural authority, we may repair to the authority of our own conscience and discover what life is all about. [142]

Thought Seven: The idea that we will lose our morals when we no longer believe in god is simply ludicrous. The very idea that we humans cannot and will not be good without god does not stand up to either historical or contemporary scrutiny. Further, it is an insult to all humans throughout time who consider themselves responsible to their fellow humans, including husbands to wives, wives to husbands, employers to employee, employees to employers, friends to friends, or neighbors to neighbors. Certainly we are all aware that there is much evil in interpersonal, public, and corporate conduct, but to claim that the state of affairs is better with an omnipotent god lurking above us makes no logical sense, especially when we face the continuing prospect of people killing each other in the name of that god or in the name of a particular religious belief. Unfortunately, we have allowed, and we continue to allow, the god belief to trump the best ethical precepts known to humankind.

Thought Eight: I stated at the end of Chapter 7 that I see the dethronement of god as the greatest hope for humankind. I believe that only when god dies do we have a fighting chance to mature and grow up. In other words, belief in god

---

142 Personal correspondence from Mary Brennan Miller: "In his commentary on the Second Vatican Council's document, *Gaudium et Spes*, Joseph Ratzinger, now Pope Benedict XVI, said: 'Over the pope...there still stands one's own conscience, which must be obeyed before all else, if necessary, even against the requirements of ecclesiastical authority.'" Joseph Ratzinger became Pope XVI on April 24, 2005.

keeps us in a childlike state and prevents us from taking full and complete responsibility for the terrible state of the world including hunger, poverty, illness, resource depletion, and idiotic warfare in the name of Yahweh, Allah, and God.

When all gods die, perhaps we can then sit down and reason together about how to share planet earth without killing each other and enslaving nations, races, and peoples, including the enslavement and mutilation of women. When all gods die, perhaps we will at last be able to share the blessings of nature and the challenges of human existence. Until that time we must stand in the courage to be solid self, in full affirmation of our humanity and in full respect for all life.

Glossary

accountability: As used here, any situation or circumstance wherein one is held responsible for one's behavior. Sometimes a situation requires accountability of us but in many situations we hold ourselves accountable to others and to society. Accountability is often considered a part of reciprocity and self responsibility.

agnosticism: As opposed to skepticism or doubt, agnosticism literally means (Greek; *a* = without, *gnosis*, knowledge.) A true agnostic position claims that metaphysical and ontological knowledge is an impossibility. The term is attributed to Thomas H. Huxley in 1869.

angst der kreatur: The basic anxiety of the creature. Allegedly used first by Karen Horney, angst der kreatur is common to all *Homo sapiens*.

anxiety: A condition of perceived ongoing restlessness and discomfort, ranging from mild to severe, chronic to acute. Anxiety, in contrast to fear, is not necessarily related to any specific object, problem, or dilemma, but is rather described frequently as being free floating and difficult to connect to any specific event or circumstance.

a-posteriori: After experience, because of experience, as a result of experience.

a-priori: Before experience, without experience, not based on experience.

asceticism: A demeanor which is self-denying or austere, rugged and without customary pleasures and comforts.

atheist: Literally, "without god." (Greek; *a* = without; *theist* = god) A strong or positive atheist claims, "I believe there is no god." A weak or negative atheist claims, "I do not believe in god."

authority: The source of expert wisdom, belief, or knowledge proclaiming the truth of a perceived reality as being indisputable and oftentimes without error and beyond question. Reliability of a source or witness. That which is perceived as being beyond question in the exercise of power and control.

being; ontic being: Real and ultimate existence. Being is the essence of life and of living creatures and things. That which exists or can be logically inferred to exist. The nature of being itself, and hence, the nature of all existence.

belief: What a person holds to be true for himself/herself, especially concerning the phenomena of life, being, and existence. The truth of a belief often depends on the authority of the force or organization propounding the belief.

binding anxiety: An activity, behavior, or mental maneuver by which a person seeks, often unconsciously, to allay anxiety or otherwise to reduce the discomfort of anxiety by attaching it or deflecting it onto some force, belief, or activity, thus protecting one's feeling of well being.

Buddhism: A religion originating in the far east, arising from the teaching of Gautama Buddha, which professes no belief in supernatural forces such as god or gods, but holds to a way of thinking and being which accepts the suffering of life and provides pathways and meditative practices to enable one's way.

canon: A norm or guiding principle, standard, or accepted regulation. A canon may refer to a rule of law or an accepted rule of practice.

catastrophic loss: Loss of any kind and dimension which is of such serious consequence so as to affect a person's equilibrium. Catastrophic loss is due to the effect of extraordinary stressors which can be sudden, unpredictable, and overwhelming, especially when compared to the effect of more normal and gradual cumulative stressors.

categorical imperative: Immanuel Kant wished to frame a principle that was absolute. He failed, as do all absolutes. The categorical in the phrase refers to its being without conditions, hence unconditional. The imperative in the phrase refers to the implicit command, you must or you ought. The categorical has two main parts. The first part proclaims that we must choose only actions and behaviors which, in good conscience, we would be willing for all of our fellow humans to choose also. This is the principle of universalization. The second part proclaims that we must always treat our fellow humans as ends in themselves rather than as means toward an end, stated or unstated.

coherence theory of truth: Truth, according to coherence theory, is the result of two or more hypotheses or theories which arrive at similar conclusions but via different means or methods of inquiry. Hypotheses or theories displaying a logical connection or consistency in a non-conflicting manner are said to be coherent.

Confucianism: A moral and humanistic philosophy originating in ancient China and based on the teachings of Confucius.

consensus theory of truth: Truth is the result of significant agreement among witnesses, participants, or even judges. Hence, if an impressive majority of people believe in the existence of god, then it must be true that there is such a being or force. If a significant number of people believe in heaven or hell, then heaven or hell must exist.

construct: Any thought, idea, or mental creation about which a person believes intently. A construct is the end product of belief and internalization and is both conscious and unconscious, representing a person's deepest wishes and thoughts about personal realities and ontological and supernatural beliefs.

correspondence theory of truth: Truth is the result of significant agreement between the alleged "facts" of a situation or proposition and the observed reality. In this manner of reasoning, whatever interpretation fits or corresponds most adequately with the alleged facts of any given situation is deemed as being true.

courage: The ability to employ physical, mental and/or moral strength to hold fast or to press on in spite of danger, fear, anxiety, weakness, self-doubt or any other impediment to one's endeavor. Strong affirmation of oneself, especially in the face of danger and tribulation.

deism: (as opposed to theism.) The belief that there exists an impersonal, transcendent, ultimate force or prime cause that created the cosmos and its inherent potential for growth and continued existence, but without any involvement by this force with human affairs or history. The creative force or deity is transcendent but not immanent.

differentiation: As employed by Murray Bowen, differentiation refers to the extent an individual is able to separate or emotionally distance oneself from the beliefs, values, and behaviors of others within the intimate bonds of family and/ or early caretakers without abandoning, absenting, or otherwise withdrawing from meaningful relationship with the family or early caretakers.

élan vital: From the philosophy of Henri-Louis Bergson, an unseen force and vital impulse, sometimes posited as the power and force of nature, biology, physiology, and physics.

empathy: A feeling into the situation, plight, or dilemma of another, be she/he an individual or a group or class of people.

Empathy, as used here, is a necessary condition for ethical behavior because it introduces the element of deep caring and concern for one's fellow human beings.

empiricism: An approach to the study of life and existence based on observed observation and experimentation without appeal to a-prior beliefs or premises. The philosophical opposite to empiricism is rationalism.

epistemology: The study of how human beings acquire knowledge, i.e., via empiricism, rationalism, revelation, consensus, or intuition. How do we know the method by which we attain knowledge is valid, and how do we know if it yields truth? How do we know what we believe we know?

essence: That which makes something what it is in its very core. The inward, intrinsic, fundamental nature of something. When one asks, "What is its essence?" the implication is that there is a unique and purposeful meaning at the heart of an event, situation, dilemma, or thing.

euphemism: A word or phrase that serves to reduce the sharpness or offensiveness of the event or occurrence for which it is being substituted . For instance, "death" or "dying is often referred to as passing, passing away, passing on, expiring.

exegesis: The process of careful examination of the use, grammar, translation, and critical analysis of words, phrases, and sentences, especially in understanding and translating the scriptures of the old and new testament from ancient Hebrew and Greek into English.

existentialism: Having to do with the experience of existence without reference to a god or vital force as pre-determining the meaning of that existence. Existence always precedes the purpose or meaning human beings assign to their own existence, i.e., existence precedes essence. Existentialism is often philosophically opposed to the idea that god, gods, or supernatural forces give meaning to existence, i.e., essence precedes existence.

existential vacuum: In the writing of Victor Frankl, a phrase indicating an inner emptiness, a void, which often gives rise to anxiety, malaise, and depression.

faith: One's credo or system of belief, sometimes unquestioned and accepted on authority, usually regarding beliefs about god, religion, and ecclesiastical propositions.

fear: A reaction common to humans and to living creatures which serves to alert the person or animal to the possibility of threat to one's physical, biological, or emotional well being. Anticipation or awareness of threatening danger. Fear portends danger, both immediate and longer ranged and is most always related to an identifiable object, event, situation, behavior or happening, in contrast to anxiety, which is difficult to relate to any specific threatening object.

feel-good chatter: A term coined by David Walsh to separate genuine self-esteem from a shallow and superficial use of praise.

first order truth (as opposed to second order truth): As used here, a person's self-proclaimed truth, i.e., whatever a person believes to be true is true for him or her. Any person's answers to questions of life and ultimacy, death and eternity arrived at via reason, speculation, rational inquiry, intuition, consensus, or revelation. Truth of the first order is true simply because the individual believes it to be true. Truth of the first order belongs to what Emmanuel Kant referred to as phenomena, in contrast to the noumena, the ultimate unknowable.

fusion - enmeshment: The blending or melding of two identities, persons, or forces wherein each is co-dependent upon the other and each is caught up in the emotional field of the other. As used in the psychological literature, a failure in one's ability to differentiate oneself, especially from one's parents or caretakers, siblings and collateral relations.

golden rule: Historic in every sense of the word, it has been known as the silver rule and the rule of reciprocity. It has been expressed in many forms and no single form is necessarily more correct than any other. Do unto others as you wish others would do to you.

higher criticism: Sometimes referred to as historical criticism. In the study of literature, especially sacred scriptures, the pursuit of answers to questions such as the origin, the history, the time of writing, the place, the circumstances, the characteristics, and the problems or circumstances of the implied audience. (In contrast to lower or textual criticism).

Hinduism: An Asian religion in origin, especially India, containing some Buddhist thought and associated with a view toward the sacredness of life. Contains mystical contemplation and the concept of dharma, the cosmic order and natural law which applies to all creation.

immanent (as opposed to transcendent): An event or occurrence which is either immediately upon the scene or is about to happen. In theology, the term refers to a deity present and active within the affairs of human beings, communities, and nations. Immanence implies a presence within the self, the community, the social order, or the larger political reality of a god, a spirit, or other supernatural force.

internalizing: The process of taking into oneself a teaching, credo, or belief and making this into a meaningful and intrinsic part of one's own personal property and possession. Internalization is a process whereby we embrace and adopt the thoughts and beliefs others would wish for us to embrace.

logotherapy: The school of psychotherapy founded and practiced by Victor Frankl deriving from his emphasis on the importance of each individual creating and finding meaning (logos) in his/her life. Frankl's 'will to meaning' is contrasted with Freud's 'will to pleasure' and Adler's 'will to power' as the basic impetus by which humans achieve mental balance and authentic selfhood.

lower criticism: Lower, or textual, criticism is a form of scholarship focusing on the texts of classical literature and scripture by rigorous examination of grammar, etymology, syntax, vocabulary, phrasing, style, spelling, and sentence construction. Lower criticism may contribute to findings related to the higher criticism, especially to questions of authorship and dating. (In contrast to higher criticism.)

metaphysics: Investigation and study of the nature of reality that is above, beyond, or after physics. Traditionally such study may include ontology, the nature of being itself, and the origin and structure of the universe. Oftentimes the word is used to indicate speculative philosophy in general.

monotheism: In the history of religion monotheism refers to the belief in one god, in contrast to polytheism.

natural theology (as opposed to revealed theology): Theological study and reasoning based on observation and study of the microcosm and macrocosm of the universe. Natural theology concerns itself with inference and deduction from the observed order or the 'natural' world rather than divine or supernatural revelations purported to be true and authentic by an authority or authority figure.

neurosis: Physical, physiological, mental, and emotional disturbance, often arising from both conscious and unconscious internal conflict. Contrary to psychosis, neurosis is not characterized as a break from reality or as a severe disturbance of one's grip on reality. Neuroses are often marked by depression, anxiety, compulsions, obsessions, and phobias. (See footnote in Chapter Two.)

nihilism: The philosophical belief in nothingness, emptiness, and meaninglessness. Usually contrasted with meaning and purpose in human existence, especially meaning and purpose that comes from without, i.e., from a god or supernatural force or spirit.

noumena: Emmanuel Kant's term, from the *nous* or mind, for the unknown and unknowable reality that is forever beyond the reach of human knowledge. The noumena, the thing in itself, is that which is apprehended by thought yet remains independent of perception by the senses. In Kantian thought noumena is contrasted with phenomena.

normative loss: Distinguished from catastrophic loss by scholars, normative loss is loss that results from the day by day living of life and the physiological, biological, and anatomical developmental processes.

omnipotent: All powerful. Usually in reference to a god or deity.

omnipresent: All present. Usually in reference to a god or deity.

omniscient: All knowing. Usually in reference to a god or deity.

placebo: A sugar pill. A pill that looks to be medicinal but in fact contains only sugar. The placebo effect is the result of the patient or client thinking that the pill has medicinal value when, in fact, it does not. In scientific experiments a placebo is often given to the control group in order that the effects, after a designated period of time, may be compared to an experimental group which has received authentic medication. If and when the control group does very well in comparison to the experimental group the experimenter usually concludes that when people believe they are being treated in an authentic manner they will respond in a positive direction, thus confirming the power of belief.

plenipotentiary: A person, usually a diplomat, invested with full power to act in place of or at the behest of the authorizing agent or government.

polytheism: Belief in two or more gods simultaneously, usually with different gods having responsibility for various functions or purposes.

pragmatic theory of truth: A theory of truth which is based on utilitarianism and general usefulness, based on the premise that if something works it must be true. The test of truth is, according to philosophical pragmatism, is based on the practical consequences of belief. (Adherents include John Dewey, Jeremy Bentham, and John Stuart Mill.)

pseudo self: A false self. A pseudo self may be either conscious or unconscious, or both. According to Bowen's *Family System Theory*, the pseudo self is not authentic nor is it based on genuine feedback. A pseudo self may be a pretend self or it may be the result of the tendency to believe we are somehow better than or superior to other people. The pseudo self maybe thought of as a persona, not the real thing. In Bowen theory, pseudo self is contrasted with solid self.

psychosis: A mental condition wherein the subject is determined to be in severe separation or disconnect with reality. Psychosis is characterized by hallucinations, delusions, and a disorganization of thought, speech, and behavior.

rationalism: A method of inquiry independent of experience in which the tools of reason and deductive logic are applied to problems not otherwise subject to direct observation and experimentation. As opposed to a-posteriori oriented empiricism, rationalism is oriented to the a-priori.

rationalization: To cause something to appear to be reasonable. Producing and providing reasons for decisions and behavior which, while plausible, are not the primary or true motive for decisions and behaviors.

radical constructivism: A name given to the philosophical/ psychological belief referring to the inability of the human organism to know or to perceive reality in any direct manner. Consequently, what one believes to be reality is an invention, a creation, or a construct of the human mind. Constructivists do not deny the existence of reality. However, they deny that reality can ever be known directly. Constructivists believe that all knowledge is perceived indirectly through the interaction of our biophysical systems, our sensory perceptions, and our mental reasoning, as these processes combine to make sense of our personal experiences. The end result is the creation of mental constructs that then become one's personal realities.

reality: Reality is what people think is accurate and factual about all life and creation. The essential question about reality is whose reality are we talking about, my reality or your reality? The never-ending question in philosophy is the epistemological question, "How is reality known?" The most important reality question is "how do we know what we think we know?" Objectivists claim reality can be known directly. Subjectivists claim that we cannot know reality directly, but only through the agency of the mind which processes sense experience interacting with the experiences of everyday life. (In philosophy, the three British empiricists, Locke, Berkeley, and Hume are classified as empiricists and subjectivists. Immanuel Kant is perhaps the most famous rationalist and objectivist, although he attempted to reconcile the two positions in his *Critique of Pure Reason.*)

reciprocity: The condition or situation wherein one returns or exchanges an object, act, favor, or kindness in balanced measure in proportion to what one has received. It is often considered a part of exchange theory.

religion: From the Latin word *ligare*, to tie or to bind. Religion may be broadly defined as how one sees oneself as being tied to the universe. Religion is popularly defined as the system of doctrine and beliefs humans hold about god or gods, the creation of the universe, and the reality or non-reality of life beyond death. Religion is also defined by the practices and socio-cultural customs devotees and adherents celebrate.

repression: (in contrast to suppression.) An unconscious process whereby the mind causes certain details of memory to be blurred or lost. Repression represents a largely involuntary exclusion from consciousness of painful and unwelcome desires, feelings, behaviors, and thoughts. Repression is to be distinguished from *suppression* which is a deliberately conscious attempt to push down or forget memories that are particularly painful, frightening, or unpleasant.

revealed theology: (as opposed to natural theology.) Knowledge about god is the direct result of god making itself known to humanity and creation. Revealed theology claims that humankind can only know god if and when god chooses to reveal itself, i.e., make itself known. Hence, divine or supernatural self-revelation of deity.

revelation: As used theologically, any supernatural showing or displaying of divine persona, spirit, directives, or information. A showing of something that was previously hidden from view. From Latin *revelare*, to uncover or to pull back the curtain.

second great commandment: As used here, the second great commandment refers to Jesus' admonition, Thou shalt love they neighbor as thyself. This command fails to rate above level four on Lawrence Kohlberg's hierarchy of moral/ethical motivational stages because the reference point is oneself.

second order truth (as opposed to first order truth): Truth of the second order is absolute truth, i.e., the way things are in absolute reality, having nothing to do with human perception or interpretation. Second order truth is impossible to attain because it transcends the limits of human knowledge and perception. Second order truth is the ultimate truth about reality and the origin of the universe. Many people tend to elevate their first order truth into second order truth via faith and religious affirmation, thus claiming their truth as being universal or their religion as being the only true faith.

self: Defined variously by different schools of philosophical and psychological thought, the self is considered to be the melding of matter, mind, spirit, emotions, and soul which in total configuration constitute the character, identity, and individuality of a person.

self-affirmation: The ability to hold forth oneself in a positive manner and resist all attempts to lose one's individuality via fusion or absorption into another in a co-dependent or symbiotic relationship.

self-assertion: The ability to press oneself forward as being worthy and unique, and thus deserving of respect. To stand up for oneself and resist attempts by others to control you or to have sway over you in any manner. To protect and defend your own life space from intrusion or manipulation by others.

self-esteem: Holding oneself as being worthy and of value both because of who you are and what you are capable of being and doing. Love for oneself in terms of positive self-regard and self-respect, resisting attempts by others to denigrate or otherwise cast aspersion on your selfhood.

Shintoism: The indigenous national religion of Japan holding the emperor as being in the line of divinity. Shintoism is an expression of reverence for one's ancestors, ancient heroes, including worship of nature and natural surroundings.

skepticism: To hold an attitude of doubt. To be dubious about claims to truth and authenticity. Doubt and the array of questions one may have concerning any number of beliefs, alleged events, and happenings. Sometimes defined incorrectly as agnosticism.

solid self: In Bowen theory, a term intended to contrast with false self or pseudo-self, indicating an autonomous, inner-directed individual with a strong sense of self-affirmation and self-assertion. Solid self indicates a well grounded identity with resolute purpose and sense of integrity in inter-personal relationships.

spiritualism: A term referring to the non-physical realm of nature. A supernatural being or essence with both benign and malevolent valences. Referring to the life of the soul in contrast to the body and its materialistic endeavors and concerns. For many it is related to a sense of divinity and for others a sense of being at one with the *ruach* or breath of life in all its possible dimensions.

suppression (in contrast to repression): A conscious attempt to push aside (usually) unpleasant or negative feelings, emotions, events, and happenstances. The end goal is avoidance or denial so that one is not bothered by negativity in any form. Suppression can also refer to the resisting of positive drives and emotions.

tabula rasa: A term from the philosophy of John Locke wherein he defends the proposition that at birth the human infant has a brain or mind that is like a blank slate, a *tabula rasa,* waiting to be written upon with the sense perceptions and experience of life. An empty state before receiving any impressions of any kind from any source.

theism (as opposed to deism): Belief in a supreme being, usually monotheistic, which is considered to be the author of the universe, supreme ruler, transcendent, immanent, omnipresent, omniscient, and omnipotent. A theistic god may be prayed to in confession, supplication, intercession, supplication, thanksgiving, and petition.

theodicy: The problem of evil while holding to a belief in an omnipotent god. (The epigraph of this work attributed to Epicurus is an example of theodicy.)

transcendent (as opposed to immanent): In theology, a transcendent being, god, or force, from across the span of space and time, throughout the galaxies of the universe, being the sustaining force of creation.

truth: See correspondence theory of truth and coherence theory of truth.

truthfulness: A trait of character in which one attempts to incorporate a straightforwardness without deception in dealings with other human beings as well as with others in the marketplace, industry, and corporations.

undifferentiated family ego mass: A term used by Murray Bowen in his family systems theory referring to the fusion and enmeshment of family members, being held together by an emotional bond or glue which serves to prevent autonomy and separation, and hence differentiated emotional identity. The greater the degree of differentiation the more likely the individual will develop solid self. The less the degree of differentiation the greater the likelihood of the development of pseudo self with increased enmeshment and fusion among parents and siblings, which then characterizes all family interaction and communication.

universalism: As used herein this term implies equal and equitable application of the same code of ethics to all classes and sub-classes of an entity, country, nation, society, or culture.

BIBLIOGRAPHY

Anderson, Elizabeth. "If God Is Dead, Is Everything Permitted?" In, *The Portable Atheist: Essential Readings for the Nonbeliever.* Philadelphia: The DeCapo Press, 2007.

Armstrong, Karen. *A History of God.* New York: Alfred A. Knopf, 1994.

Becker, Ernest. *The Denial of Death.* New York: The Free Press, 1973.

Barker, Dan. *Godless: How An Evangelical Preacher Became One of America's Leading Atheists.* Berkeley, California: Ulysses Press, 2008.

Bowen, Murray. *Family Therapy In Clinical Practice.* New York: Jason Aronson, 1978.

Church, Forrest. *Love and Death.* Boston: Beacon Press. 2008.

Crosby, John F. *The Flipside of Godspeak: Theism As Constructed Reality.* Eugene, Oregon: Wipf &Stock, 2007.

"Theories of Anxiety: A Theoretical Perspective." The *American Journal of Psychoanalysis* 36:237-248.

Dawkins, Richard. *The God Delusion*: Boston: Houghton Mifflin Company, 2006

Epstein, Greg. *Good Without God: What A Billion Nonreligious People Do Believe.* New York: Harper Collins, 2009.

Figley, Charles R., and Hamilton McCubbin *Stress and the Family,* Volume I, *Coping With Normative Transitions* and Volume II, *Coping With Catastrophe.* New York: Brunner/Mazel, 1983.

Frankl, Victor. *The Doctor and the Soul: From Psychotherapy to Logotherapy.* New York: Alfred A. Knopf, Inc. 1946.

—— *Man's Search For Meaning.* Boston: Beacon Press. Washington Square Press Edition, 1963. (Originally published as: *From Death Camp to Existentialism,* 1959.)

Freud, Sigmund. *The Future of an Illusion.* New York: The Free Press, 1927.

Fromm, Erich. *Escape From Freedom.* New York: Holt, Rinehart, and Winston, 1941.

Funk, Robert W., and Roy W. Hoover, and The Jesus Seminar. *The Five Gospels: The Search for the Authentic Words of Jesus.* New York: The Polebridge Press, Macmillan Publishing Company, 1993.

Gilligan, Carol. *In a Different Voice: Psychological Theory and Women's Development.* Cambridge, Massachusetts: Harvard University Press, 1982.

Glasersfeld, Ernst von. *Radical Constructivism: A Way of Knowing and Learning.* New York: RoutledgeFalmer, 1995.

Harris, Richard. *The End of Faith: Religion, Terror, and the Future of Reason.* New York: W. W. Norton and Company, 2004.

Hitchens, Christopher. *god is Not Great: How Religion Poisons Everything.* New York: Hachette Book Group USA, 2007.

Horney, Karen. *The Neurotic Personality of Our Time.* New York: W. W. Norton & Company, 1937

Kant, Immanuel. *Groundwork of the Metaphysics of Morals.* New York: Cambridge University Press, 1998. (Cambridge Texts in the History of Philosophy.) (Kant 1724-1804)

Kerr, Michael, and Murray Bowen. *Family Evaluation : An Approach Based On Bowen Theory.* New York: W. W. Norton & Company, 1988.

Kohlberg, Lawrence. *The Philosophy of Moral Development.* New York: Harper & Row, 1981.

Kopp, Sheldon B. *If You Meet the Buddha On the Road, Kill Him: The Pilgrimage of Psychotherapy Patients.* Palo Alto, California: Science and Behavior Books, 1972.

May, Rollo. *The Meaning of Anxiety.* New York: The Ronald Press, 1950.

——*Power and Innocence: A Search For the Sources of Violence.* New York: W.W. Norton & Company, 1972.

Niebuhr, Reinhold. *Moral Man and Immoral Society: A Study of Ethics and Politics.* New York: Charles Scribner's Sons, 1932.

Paley, William. *Natural Theology: Or Evidences of the Existence and Attributes of the Deity, Collected From the Appearances of Nature.* Boston: Gould and Lincoln, 1860 Edition.

Satir, Virginia. *The New Peoplemaking*. Mountain View, California: Science and Behavior Books, 1988.

Spong, John Shelby. *Why Christianity Must Change or Die: A Bishop Speaks To Believers In Exile*. San Francisco: HarperSanFrancisco, 1998

Tillich, Paul. *The Courage To Be*. New Haven: The Yale University Press, 1952.

Young, Julian. *The Death of God and the Meaning of Life*. London and New York: Routledge, Taylor & Francis Group, 2003.

Walsh, David. *No: Why Kids — of All Ages — Need To Hear It and Ways Parents Can Say It*. New York: The Free Press, 2007.

INDEX